GUIDEBOOK

FOR THE

YOUNG OFFICER

ISBN-13 978-0-9831745-5-4

ISBN-10 0-9831745-9-8

1st edition, 2011

Previously Published as "Guidebook for the Young Air Defense Officer"

Published by:

121 Castle Drive STE F
Madison, AL 35758
info@mentorenterprisesinc.com

Special thanks to SFC Mackie Ocampo for contributing to the promotions section

The man who is self-seeking never becomes a real leader.
The time inevitably comes when the self-seeking leader
fails to inspire confidence, and the moment a leader
fails to inspire confidence he ceases to be a leader.

—Brig. Gen. A. L. Singleton

DEDICATION

This book is dedicated to all battery and company commanders, past, present and future. For when the U.S. Army deploys to combat, the majority of the units directly confronting the adversary belong to the battery and company commanders. All other headquarters support, plan or realign forces contributing to the battlefield framework. Battery and company commanders are the real leaders/warfighters.

I add a special thanks and dedication to my first battery commander who, years ago, made such a strong impression on me. I start this book with a short description of this remarkable man with the hope that you see a little of yourself in him.

–*FJC*

The Battery Commander

His average build does not impress you, but his oversized head and hands can make him look like a menacing creature when he is angry. His deep set eyes, prominent nose and large, light brown eyebrows contribute to the overall effect. Luckily, as my first commander and mentor in the U.S Army, his normal persona is actually jovial and fatherly. For a young officer wanting to succeed, he is an outstanding role model.

He leads by example. His green fatigue uniform is always smartly pressed with creases in the shirt centered over his left and right pockets, making him look slimmer and taller than his 6-foot, 175-pound frame. His highly shined combat boots reflect so much light you can see your reflection from a few feet away. Placed on his head is an olive-green baseball cap with the silver railroad track rank insignia of a captain. His facial expression displays an unwavering sense of determination and duty. He knows what his mission entails, and he fulfills that mission with a passion rarely recorded in the modern Army.

Conversing with him can be both a punishing and uplifting experience. In either case, the Soldier automatically receives the respect and appreciation of his position. His directness and honesty can be disconcerting until you understand he's that way with everyone. Soldiers feel comfortable talking to the captain because they now him to be a tough but fair individual who shows appreciation for outstanding results. The opposing aspect of his personality is fairly predictable—poor performance equals loss of privileges. The key to his demeanor is that his orders are clear and consistent. Everyone knows what results he wishes to attain in any exercise or operation. When the unit succeeds, he always shares that success with everyone in the unit, providing positive strokes for all deserving souls. Those individuals that fail the unit are promptly punished or removed from active service. Many times I've heard him say, "In the game of war, winning is all that counts."

His role as mentor and friend does not stop upon your departure from the unit. He routinely calls to inquire about one of his "sons." His inquiry routinely includes a positive statement about the successes we enjoyed together, making me feel appreciated. At the end of the telephone conversation he often tries to cite something positive like, "You're golden, I wish I had your abilities and potential."

Where do we get such men? That's something of a mystery, but no one doubts the Army and the nation would soon find itself in dire straits without them. History and the fortunes of war may never place my first battery commander's name, Captain (now Colonel(R)) Dana F. Kwist, alongside those of MacArthur, Eisenhower, Patton or Schwarzkopf, but it is Soldiers such as he who make the Army a meaningful and exhilarating profession. His ability to motivate and generate loyalty from subordinates is unmatched. My respect and admiration for him are unbounded. I would work for him anywhere, anytime and under the most torturous circumstances. Without his influence in my life, I would not have chosen a career in the U.S. Army. I thank God for this man.

TABLE OF CONTENTS

FOREWORD

When I was a LTC at Fort Bliss, Texas, I wrote, and the Army published, my first officer training book. This book covered my 9 rules for young military leaders. These rules were my own concoction based on years of leadership experience. At the time, I thought they were common sense rules and not particularly insightful. However, as officers, we never know the positive effect we might have on a person. Let me tell you about one such encounter with a civilian employee. I call the story:

Rule Number 7

My new officers training book was being sold at the Air Defense Museum and other locations on Fort Bliss, Texas. One day I walked into the Air Defense museum to attend a meeting when the cashier at the front display case stopped me and said, "You are Colonel Caravella, aren't you?"

I stopped, turned and said, "Yes, ma'am, I am. How may I help you?"

The cashier was in her mid-40's, black hair with a large gray streak in the front portions of her pony-tailed hair. Her frumpy body stooped over like a person with a degenerative back disease. She looked at me and said with a stern voice, "Rule Number 7."

My face turned a little red as I said, "Ma'am, I know I wrote the 9 rules for leaders, but at the moment I can't remember which one was number 7."

The cashier turned back to a chair in which a copy of my book lay with a large white piece of paper marking a specific page. She grabbed the book and prepared herself like a great oratory prepping for a major speech. She unfurled her hair, shook her head left and right, then opened the book in front of her and assumed the position of attention with head forward, shoulders back and feet together. The frumpy cashier, who I first met, had transformed herself into a person of fortitude. With determination, she read, "Rule Number 7. Believe in yourself. If you don't, why should anybody else?" This transformed person stepped forward and offered her hand. She shook my hand vigorously and added, "You don't know what your words meant to me." Her unexpected response touched my heart.

You, young officer, have significant influence and power to mold and grow people under your command. You can touch their hearts in ways yet to be learned. My goal is that this book helps you on that journey of fruitful leadership no matter what your final career choice might be.

CHAPTER ONE

So you want to be an Army Lieutenant

Repeatedly you've heard the term leader of men as it pertains to second lieutenants. All new young lieutenants understand their eventual role, but they all start out with some gnawing questions that attack their self-confidence. What should I do first as a lieutenant? How should I act, etc.? In this section of the book, I will address those questions and more. You don't have to agree with my assertions or points, but I hope that my questions and answers spawn some forethought on the subjects so that you start your leadership career with a sense of balance and minimum anxiety. This chapter uses a question and answer format with the questions being derived from my personal interactions with numerous lieutenants.

What is the first thing I should do as a lieutenant before reporting to my first leadership position?

Without a doubt, every new lieutenant worries about that first impression upon arriving at his new unit. There are, however, a few precursory comments that need to be made before answering the main question at hand.

Lieutenant, trust in your training and judgment. You have already established yourself as an individual who possesses the capabilities to lead. Not everyone is so fortunate. Your accomplishment of earning a commission provides evidence of your potential. Of course, you still have much to learn, but you already possess the tools to succeed.

While assessing the 40+ lieutenants who have worked for me over the years, I've found that two criteria were enough to divide them into their respective potential categories. The first category is cognitive ability. Bluntly put, this is brain power—and some individuals possess more than others. However, not everyone knows how to apply their God-given intellectual faculties. This point leads to the next category, which I can describe in one word: will. Some of the most talented people in the world accomplish little because they lack the will to use their talents. Remember, in the end, obtaining results is the most important aspect of any profession. Most senior leaders will tell you that they will take a young lieutenant with average talent and a large motivation factor over an exceptionally talented lieutenant who just goes through the motions.

My point in this discussion is that motivation and results are more important to successful leadership than pure talent. The world is overflowing with people who never reach their personal potential. In almost all cases, their failure relates to their lack of will.

In addressing the main question, you should first contact your new company commander by telephone before arriving at the unit and tell him how fortunate you are drawing an assignment to his unit. Profess your eagerness to learn and work.

The next step is reporting to the unit. Make sure your uniform fits properly and pay proper respect to all senior leaders that you meet. When you finally meet your company commander, keep your discussion straightforward and honest. If you don't know something, say so. There are a few questions you need answered by the company commander before you leave this first meeting to avoid starting your platoon time in the wrong direction:

What is the mission of the company and how does my platoon contribute to that mission? He should be able to give you specific tasks that you will be able to study later.

What is the company commander's assessment of the platoon and platoon sergeant? Also, will any near-term personnel changes significantly affect platoon readiness?

What routine duties will I be expected to accomplish?

Does an officer professional development ladder exist in the battalion? Good battalions have an officer development program that addresses this subject in detail. Know what the ladder is for your unit and move up it.

How do I relate to my platoon sergeant?

This question also begets a few comments of philosophy before directly addressing the issue. Leader-subordinate relationships have been researched ad infinitum. Best-sellers come out every year addressing the "latest" and "best" approach to motivating and guiding one's subordinates. But I can simplify situational leadership by adopting four different approaches, depending on the type of follower that works for you. My four categories of subordinates are:

Type 1: Highly motivated with a gifted cognitive ability.

Type 2: Highly motivated with little to average talent.

Type 3: Poorly motivated with a gifted cognitive ability.

Type 4: Poorly motivated with little ability.

The first requirement relating to our platoon sergeant is to determine which of the four types you've drawn. Once you've made an assessment, act according to that type. My guidance on how to interact with each type is cited below:

If you happen to have a Type 1 platoon sergeant, you are blessed. Give this platoon sergeant general guidance about the standards you expect. Give him the leeway to prepare and train the platoon while you participate and inspect. Yes, inspect. Good platoon sergeants want the platoon leader to inspect the troops in garrison, the motor pool and the field.

A Type 2 platoon sergeant can operate successfully but requires more specific guidance by the platoon leader. Once this platoon sergeant understands the mission, he will do the right things to accomplish the mission. Please remember that platoon sergeants do not generally have the skills to formulate and execute operations orders to the same degree as lieutenants. This flaw usually shows up during the sustained operations area of a unit.

Of all situational leadership types, Type 3 is quite an enigma. It's hard to understand why talented people fail to execute and achieve, but in my experience the main reason is laziness. For example, if your platoon sergeant has been around for some time and has not been promoted to master sergeant, there is probably a good reason. Some individuals start to "retire" while on active duty, causing a significant problem for the unit. This platoon sergeant is a poor example for the young NCOs and Soldiers, and causes the platoon's training efficiency to suffer. This platoon sergeant type will get his men killed in combat. The young, green platoon leader must prevent this potential catastrophe. You prevent it by finding a way to motivate this platoon sergeant or by relieving him for cause. There are no other courses of action. Written counseling along with positive verbal strokes and encouragement are all the tools the platoon leader has open to him in the short term. The worst choice for a platoon leader is to do nothing. If the platoon sergeant fails to respond, the platoon leader's only option is to bring his case to the company commander and battalion command sergeant major. Ninety-nine percent of the time, the problem disappears at that level. However, if it doesn't, don't be afraid to carry the issue to the battalion commander. You owe it to your Soldiers.

Concerning all Type 4 NCOs—don't waste your time on them. Counsel them solely for the purpose of eliminating them from the U.S. Army.

You have an obligation to help an NCO in need. But when you've done everything for him you can, it's time for him to find a new profession. This may seem a little cruel, but it's not. This type of NCO lacks skills and is no longer happy serving his country. That's OK. He is better off somewhere else where he doesn't affect your unit readiness. Lieutenant, one of the reasons you get paid the bigger dollars is to make the tough, but necessary decisions.

What are the most important things for me to know and learn?

Of course, the exact answers to this question will vary somewhat depending on your unit mission. But there are a few fundamental elements that every lieutenant should understand. Basic equipment knowledge and deployment fundamentals are vital to mission accomplishment. Most lieutenants take about six months to fully acquaint themselves with their assigned weapons systems and support equipment; i.e., radios, antennas, trucks, etc.

Some never accomplish this task and their credibility becomes weak within the company, and more importantly, with their supported units. The only way to avoid falling into this unfortunate category is by admitting you don't know all the answers and asking someone who does for help. Don't be afraid of losing face. As the following scene described by one of Napoleon's junior officers demonstrates, truly great leaders know the importance of mastering the most minute details of their profession and are not averse to learning from their subordinates.

"I happened to be at the office of the general staff in the Rue Neuve des Capucines when General Bonaparte came in. I can still see the little hat, surmounted by a pick-up plume, his coat cut anyhow, and a sword which, in truth, did not seem the sort of weapon to make anyone's fortune. Flinging his hat on a large table in the middle of the room, he went up to an old general named Krieg, a man with a wonderful knowledge of detail and the author of a very good Soldiers' manual. He made him take a seat beside him at the table and began questioning him, pen in hand, about a host of facts connected with the service and discipline. Some of his questions showed such a complete ignorance of

some of the most ordinary things that several of my comrades smiled. I was myself struck by the number of his questions, their order and their rapidity, no less than by the way in which the answers were caught up, and often found to resolve into other questions, which he deduced in consequence from them. But what struck me still more was the sight of a commander-in-chief perfectly indifferent about showing his subordinates how completely ignorant he was of the various points of a business which the youngest of them was supposed to know perfectly, and this raised him a thousand cubits in my opinion."

You may find learning the "nuts and bolts" of your branch weaponry, equipment and operations tedious, but in the long run, getting it down requires far less time and effort than continually concealing your lack of knowledge. Time spent camouflaging a lack of technical expertise is, at any rate, wasted time, for this defect sooner or later becomes obvious to everyone.

No one needs to understand the special requirements of your weapon systems more than you do. The battalion or brigade task force commander looks to you for advice. Don't be afraid to voice your concerns on deployment and special system maintenance requirements.

Every division in the Army has its specified and implied missions. You must personally understand those missions and how they impact on your platoon. For example, many divisions require a deployment ready battalion (DRB) to be on notice for an 18-hour deployment anywhere in the world. How do you fit into the DRB package? What kind of load do you normally prepare your platoon to take in the ready line? Who supplies your ammunition, both small arms and missile related?

You must have answers to these questions (and more) and preplan the contingencies. There isn't enough time to find out the answers to deployment questions once the alarm rings.

So to specifically answer the main question, company grade officers must learn unit procedures and equipment operation. They must understand standing operating procedures (SOPs) to the letter. All routine platoon operations must specifically support unit SOPs and all unit raining should support the unit missions.

I understand that as a young lieutenant, you may not grasp exactly what I'm addressing at this point, but don't fret. If you arrive at your first duty station with the right questions, the right answers will soon follow. Your time and efforts will be fruitful in the long term which usually results in a platoon leader achieving success.

One other aspect of personal training demands discussion: Army schools. Generally, I would say that the more Army schools a lieutenant attends the better it is for both the officer and the Army. The typical schools for a young officer may be motor maintenance; air and rail load; nuclear, biological and chemical; airborne; air assault; ranger; etc. The exact schools required depend on your unit mission. Given the smaller competitive Army of tomorrow, the young aggressive officer with multiple skills has a decided advantage over his contemporaries.

When and how should I inspect?

The answer to this common question depends greatly on the type of platoon sergeant you possess (as discussed earlier). However, there are a few basic rules that every lieutenant should understand. These are my personal rules relating to inspections based on my experiences as both a company and field grade officer.

Rule 1: Inspect everything, constantly.

Rule 2: Conduct both announced and unannounced inspections.

Rule 3: Give clear guidance for each inspection so that the troops understand exactly what you are looking for.

Rule 4: Understand the items or procedures you're inspecting. If you don't, make it known that you wish to learn as well as inspect. Your subordinates will go out of their way to show you the correct procedures or item. This approach usually enhances platoon morale because it shows the lieutenant cares about the Soldier's job and wants to understand the specifics of it. Without question, this approach improves job gratification for the young trooper.

Rule 5: Whenever you find above-standard performance, praise the effort. Letters of commendation from the company commander or the battalion commander carry significant weight with the Soldier. Don't be shy in this area; Praise! Praise! Praise! when deserved.

Rule 6: At the other end of the spectrum, after inspecting ensure that you correct substandard performance. There are a number of ways to accomplish this. From my experience, I would recommend that the lieutenant just have the squad or section correct the requirement until the standard is reached. Make sure you don't let them go home until the standard is achieved. The squad learns a heavy but beneficial lesson when you demand high standards and will accept nothing less. Expect complaints, but in their hearts, the troops love a lieutenant with high standards.

Rule 7: You are the standard setter in your platoon. Do not delegate this requirement unless you're under unusual circumstances. For a limited time only, you may entrust a subordinate.

The first sergeant and I never seem to be working together. How can he and I work together better?

Frankly, if you have a problem with the first sergeant, the first place you turn is to your platoon sergeant. The platoon sergeant understands the routine duties the first sergeant must complete, and he should take these into account during your everyday activity. You, as a young lieutenant, must understand that the first sergeant's loyalties are to the company commander. He will do anything, at the expense of subordinate's desires, if required, to satisfy his boss. Have no fear; there is a way around this issue for a young lieutenant. Sit down with the first sergeant and have a short man-to-man session. Make sure your platoon sergeant is present. Tell the first sergeant what training goals you would like to accomplish, and provide him the specific dates, times, etc. You will find that most first sergeants will go out of their way to appease you as long as you agree to address a few problems in his area. In the end, the company and platoon sergeants look better for combining their collective efforts, and the company commander will notice your mature approach to diverse requirements.

What should I put in my platoon leader's notebook?

Every young leader needs critical data concerning his organization and people at his fingertips to make timely and informed decisions. Given the pace at which some units operate, the best lieutenants maintain a platoon leader's notebook that assists them in their most important tasks. Now let's get to the point and my recommendations for you on this issue.

Section 1: The most important item in your platoon notebook relates to your Soldiers. You must have daily accountability. You should know where your Soldiers are at all times. For example, you should know that a Soldier went to the dental clinic, emergency leave, ordinary leave, special details, etc. I'm not saying that you must personally give permission for these absences, but you should possess the information so that you can take appropriate action if necessary. Make sure you include personal information on each Soldier as well. Look below for my example.

John Doe

MOS, Rank, Date of Rank

Date eligible for next promotion

Civilian schooling level

Marital status, number of dependents and their names

Required schooling (military and civilian; i.e., GED)

Home address and phone number, if applicable

Reenlistment eligibility date

I find that weak platoon leaders, without exception, cannot account for their personnel. This weakness is the precursor to major failure in the platoon.

Section 2: The second important inclusion in the notebook is the statement of your major mission. This may seem somewhat elemental, but many young officers do not understand the "most" important results he must attain.

Section 3: What are the major collective tasks your platoon must be proficient in to accomplish the mission? List these tasks with a date denoting the last time the platoon practiced them.

Section 4: Have a listing of the current wartime battle crews for your weapons systems. Note who falls under what squad leader and the length of time these crews have been working together. Also list individual permanent-change-of-station dates by the Soldiers' names. It's a known fact that crews who work together longer are more proficient and perform better in combat.

Section 5: Equipment mission status requires daily monitoring. List every item of equipment assigned to your platoon on a typed chart covered with acetate. Update this chart with requisition and work order numbers as appropriate.

Section 6: If the battalion has an officer professional development checklist, include it. Make sure it's updated to reflect your accomplishments and goals.

Section 7: Lastly, place a quick reference phone listing of your most important numbers. This list usually grows over time.

What rewards and punishment do I have available to me as a lieutenant?

The answers to this question vary considerably. But from a regulatory standpoint, you have wide latitude in addressing personnel issues.

Not all personnel actions are bad. However, in my experience, most of the positive personnel actions do not happen without a good leader's intervention or initiative. This means you and the platoon sergeant are the catalysts.

To address disciplinary problems at the platoon leader level, the most important tool is the written counseling statement. If issued in conjunction with a verbal counseling, the written counseling statement is an effective mechanism to change most Soldiers' behavior.

But, of course, there are always a few Soldiers who prefer to be mavericks. These Soldiers fail to listen to or follow instructions or procedures. These Soldiers inevitably get someone killed in either a training accident or combat. Extra training by the chain of command is usually the best route to take with these Soldiers. Impress on them that they are going to be part of the team and that all team members must meet minimum standards. I've found that a Soldier's time is more precious to him than his money. Use this hammer wisely.

Your next direct tool to change irresponsible behavior is the summary Article 15. Use this non-judicial punishment for minor offenses that usually result in the Soldier performing some extra duty. Remember, extra duty and extra training are not the same. Extra duty is a punishment while extra training is just what it professes to be, additional training for the purpose of meeting a standard. I'll discuss this in detail later in the chapter.

Where should I place myself during the work day? What would be most productive?

Again, the answer to this question is not straightforward because so many things are personality dependent. But I will give you my ideas on the basic fundamentals of what a lieutenant should be doing on an average day.

Immediately after accountability formation and physical training, quickly remind your subordinate leaders of the day's training goals and provide any last minute guidance.

Following personal hygiene, check in with the company commander to confirm with him your day's activities and to receive any last minute guidance or information. This is the time that you will usually find out about visitors from inside and outside the command.

Just prior to the company work formation, walk through several barracks rooms that belong to your platoon. Whether you find deficiencies or not, report your findings to your platoon sergeant. You want him to know that you care about the living conditions of your troops. Your actions suggest to the men that you demand high standards in all areas.

This brings me to a good point to talk about a pet peeve of mine. I tell all my subordinates to do all routine things in a platoon routinely. This might sound a little dumb to you, but think about it, this saying makes sense. Platoons that maintain high standards on routine items waste little precious training time. This also promotes an enhanced disciplinary environment. So no matter what you check, like barracks rooms, insist routine tasks be executed in a routine outstanding manner. Now back to your work day.

For the daily programmed training, as a minimum, you present yourself at the start. YOU should participate if the training is on skills that you need to learn or refresh yourself on. Don't be a know-it-all. Your participation sends a message to the troops that their job skills are important and that the lieutenant isn't too proud to get his hands dirty.

If other duties require you to leave for a time, make it be known that you will inspect the platoon on that day's training. Make sure you follow through on this. Do not inspect everyone; just randomly pick a few Soldiers. You'll reinforce the lesson for that day and provide job satisfaction for your Soldiers who endeavor to learn new skills for that day.

When the training day is complete, ensure equipment is in its proper storage location in an operable condition. You must use this equipment for future training and possibly wartime. Proper maintenance is good training. Make correct maintenance a routine activity.

The day is not complete until you've done a quick verbal assessment with your subordinate leadership on their preparedness for the next day's training activities. Once assured, it's time to check in with your company commander to report on the day's activities (if he did not have a chance to check on you himself). Add to your report your planned activities for the next training day or cycle. This action builds the commander's confidence in you and also promotes a positive rapport with him.

Lastly, before leaving for home, complete any paperwork that your position entails. This usually involves additional duties that all officers must endure.

How do I recommend my Soldiers for promotion?

This is an important question that directly affects the morale and livelihood of your Soldiers. The exact methodology depends on the Soldier's rank and is covered by AR 600-8-19 (Enlisted Promotions and Reductions) and AR 614-200 (Enlisted Assignments and Utilization Management). As a consequence, I will separate the discussion in four categories: PVT–SPC, CPL, SGT–SSG and SFC.

Promotions from PVT—SPC are automatic based on time in service and time in grade. However, commanders may deny a Soldier automatic promotion if they deem the Soldier to be undeserving. Below is a table of time in service (TIS) and time in grade (TIMIG) criteria for automatic promotion up to SPC:

Promotion to	TIS	TIMIG
PV2	6 months	none
PFC	12 months	4 months
SPC	24 months	6 months

The system will automatically promote Soldiers who meet the above criteria unless the Commander denies their promotion and the Unit S1 enters a denial of promotion transaction in the personnel system (eMILPO). As with anything, Commanders must sign the Enlisted Promotions Report which validates each promotion or denial.

When your Soldier deserves early promotion, you may recommend a promotion with waiver if waivers are authorized for that month. Unit S1s calculate the number of authorized waivers per company/battalion on a monthly basis and will give the allocations to the Commanders for their use. Waivers are awarded at the Commander's discretion; not all waivers for the month have to be used. Waivers are calculated based on a certain percentage of the rank's population. For instance, waivers to PV2 and PFC cannot exceed 20 percent of the total population for those ranks. Waivers to SPC cannot exceed the SPCs waiver percentage as established monthly by HQDA which are announced on the monthly promotion cut-off scores to SGT and SSG.

Given that waivers are under a quota and can sometimes be hard to come by, your Soldier may not be the one your Commander and 1SG select to receive the waiver. If you have a high speed Soldier, it is your responsibility to convince your Commander and 1SG to move your Soldier ahead of others. Below is a table of TIS and TIG criteria for promotions with waivers up to SPC:

Promotion to	TIS	TIMIG
PV2	4 months	none
PFC	6 months	2 months
SPC	18 months	3 months

Corporal

CPLs are laterally appointed, not promoted. And unlike all other ranks that are covered by AR 600-8-19, lateral appointments to CPL are covered by AR 614-200. Commanders in the grade of O5 and above may authorize lateral appointments of SPC to CPL without a local selection board. The rule of thumb is that the Soldier must be assigned to an authorized (documented) NCO position in their CPMOS. If there is no vacant NCO slot, then you cannot recommend your Soldier for lateral appointment. When recommending a SPC for lateral appointment to CPL, ensure that the Soldier is indeed worthy of wearing junior NCO stripes and can beyond any doubt; perform the duties of an NCO. Though the most junior of all NCO ranks, wearing CPL stripes can often times prove to be more challenging than one may think.

Sergeant & Staff Sergeant

In order to get promoted to the SGT and SSG ranks, SPCs/CPLs and SGTs must appear before a promotion board which is often presided over by the unit Command Sergeant Major. Soldiers who appear before the promotion board will receive a GO/NO-GO which determines if they will be integrated onto the Promotion Standing List. There is however an exception to promotion board attendance called Command List Integration (CLI) which I will mention in the next section.

Before any Soldier can be recommended for promotion board appearance, they must meet the time requirement for promotion as of the first day of the promotion month. Soldiers are authorized to attend promotion boards from the 20th–8th of the preceding promotion month. For example, if the promotion month is August, Soldiers can attend the promotion board from 20 June to 8 July.

Below are the time requirements for promotion as of the first day of the promotion month:

Promotion to	Primary Zone		Secondary Zone	
	TIS	TIMIG	TIS	TIMIG
SSG	72	10	48	7
SGT	36	8	18	6

Once your Soldier has been recommended by the board for integration onto the promotion standing list, they will be awarded up to 800 points based on their qualifications and achievements.

Below is a breakdown of areas and how many promotion points can be earned:

Area	Promotion to SGT	Promotion to SSG
Military Training (Combat Experience, Weapons Qualification, Army Physical Fitness Test)	340	255
Awards, Decorations, & Achievements (Awards & Decorations, Badges, Certificates of Achievement, Airborne Advantage)	125	165

Military Education (NCOES, Formal Military Training, Army Correspondence Course Program)	260	280
Civilian Education (Civilian College Courses, College Level Exam Program (CLEP), Defense Activity for Non-Traditional Education Support (DANTES), Technical Certifications, Defense Language Proficiency Test (DLPT)	75	100

After your Soldier is integrated onto the Promotion Standing List and becomes promotable, it becomes a waiting game. The Army publishes the minimum number of points required for promotion to SGT and SSG monthly. Encourage your Soldier to seek more points in every way possible while waiting for cut-off scores to come out.

Command List Integration

Soldiers who meet a certain amount of TIS and TIMIG will be integrated onto the Promotion Standing List without board appearance unless denied integration by the Commander. SPCs who will meet 48 months at the time of promotion will receive a total of 39 points. SGTs who will meet 84 months at the time of promotion will receive 14 points. No additional promotion points, regardless of qualifications or achievements, will be granted unless the Soldier goes through the formal board process. Soldiers on CLI will be promoted if they belong to a Star MOS (critically short MOS). Star MOSs are published on the monthly cut-off scores for promotion to SGT and SSG. CLI Soldiers are promoted based on order of merit. Meaning, just because the cut-off score is 15 does not necessarily mean your Soldier will get promoted to SSG. The Army will identify how many slots need to be filled by Star MOS and rank and promote based on order of merit. The order of merit list goes by TIMIG and TIS, meaning those senior in grade and service get promoted first. A question I will leave for you to ponder on is... if your Soldier is truly deserving of a promotion, why not just recommend him for the promotion board instead of Command List Integration so they can garner more points?

Staff Sergeants are promoted by centralized promotion boards which are similar to officer selection boards. SFC selection boards are held at the HQDA level and select SSGs for promotion to SFC based on the board's set criteria. Centralized boards usually consist of a General Officer and Senior NCOs. Panels are divided up into branches and sometimes by MOS, depending on the population of that particular MOS. Board members individually go over the entirety of a Soldier's record to include their ERB, NCOERs and OMPF. While you have no direct influence on the board's selection process, the best thing you can do is to ensure your NCO receives an NCOER that is written as due. If you have a stellar NCO, make sure his NCOER is written well. Try to make sure every bullet is quantifiable and corresponds with the appropriate rating. For example, a score of 270 on the APFT is better reflected by an "excellence" rating than a "successful" rating. Not very many Soldiers can attain 270 on the APFT and be awarded the Army Physical Fitness Badge. Realize that the NCOER is your NCOs report card, and you want to paint a holistic picture of your NCO to board members who do not personally know your NCO and his capabilities. The NCOER may be the most important factor in determining whether an NCO has the potential to serve at the next higher grade. Do not take this responsibility lightly. Document all your Soldiers' actions so when the time comes, you are not scrounging around for data. But then again, you should be capturing all of this in your quarterly counselings anyway. In accordance with AR 623-3, all NCOERs must be reviewed by the 1SG, CSM or SGM. Take this opportunity to seek their professional guidance.

Getting promoted to any rank is not easy. As a leader, it is *your* responsibility to train, mentor, mold and allow your Soldiers to grow. Give your Soldiers a sense of responsibility and ownership, regardless of their rank. Let them surprise you! Let them shine in their own way so you can discover who is ready for increased responsibility by being recommended for promotion. Allow them sufficient time to train. Do not hold them back during ranges or APFTs to complete other tasks that can be accomplished later. Study with them for promotion boards, studying is much easier with a study partner. If time and mission permit, allow them to attend military training, complete correspondence courses and attend to civilian college courses. Lastly, never let good deeds and achievements fall through the cracks. Recommend your Soldiers for awards when recognition is due. Sit down with your Soldier to ensure he understands what he can do in order to get promoted. These are the simplest things you can do to aid the professional growth and success of your Soldier.

What is the proper way to interface with my ground task force commander?

You must realize that all ground force commanders have varying personalities and their warfighting tendencies may be different. However, each ground force commander has one common requirement concerning your particular specialty (fire support, engineer, air defense, etc). They all want to understand what the platoon leader can and cannot do with his forces on the battlefield. The ground force commander is not usually an expert in your specialty area. You are! He looks to you for recommendations in allocating your forces to best support "his" combat plan. So the first order of business with your supported ground commander, besides introducing yourself, is to brief him on your combat capabilities. He also needs to understand any special support requirements you might have. Given that some equipment is unique and maintenance intensive, this information is key for his staff guidance. How are you going to feed your troops? What about Class IX flow for your specialty related items? Brief your supported unit commander as soon as reasonably possible after taking over your platoon. This sends the message to the ground force commander that you truly are in charge of your forces and will be there when he needs you.

The second and equally important part is to listen carefully to the ground force commander's guidance and pet peeves. For example, if this commander happens to deem net control and foxhole depth important, ensure your platoon attains his standards in these areas. In many cases, I've found that support platoons exceed the ground forces units in adhering to command guidance. This attention to detail impresses the ground force commander and goes a long way toward providing a good impression of your platoon and the support community. More importantly the Soldiers in your platoon understand and desire high standards because you demand them. In the end, everyone looks good and accomplishes the mission in a coordinated, aggressive common sense manner.

How do I influence the training schedule so that I address those training tasks that I want to improve upon?

Army training professes centralized planning with decentralized execution. So for you to influence the training schedule for your platoon, you should look at and study the planning documents. In the S3 shop, you will find a 12- to 18-month long-range calendar for major events published by the major command. Read it and write down in your platoon leader's notebook the major events affecting your platoon. The S3 maintains a six-month long-range calendar, per regulations for the battalion. This plan lays out the overall contributions to higher command requirements and significant battalion commander directed events. An example of a battalion commander directed event might be a command inspection of your unit. Review both of these documents and assess your company's contributions. How is your platoon affected?

Once you've reached a few conclusions on your significant platoon requirements, you can start looking at the open dates to assess and schedule platoon training required to support the major events and to input other training exercises that you deem necessary to ensure your platoon's combat readiness.

The next obvious question is, "Where do I, as a platoon leader, submit my training requirements?" Platoon leaders submit requirements to the company commander at the unit's weekly training meeting. I advise you to consider talking to the company commander one-on-one ahead of time to ensure he understands your particular needs. This also might give you a leg up on the other lieutenants as the company commander is more likely to approve a lieutenant's plan when that lieutenant understands the mission priorities and actively pursues them with forethought. My experience has shown me that the best lieutenants have planned and resourced their training to a degree that, when execution time rolls around, their platoon reaps the best benefits and rewards. In an average battalion, I estimate that only one lieutenant per company generally plans and executes training in a high standard. These officers ultimately rate as the best in their respective companies.

Here is the question for you at this point. Which lieutenant type are you going to be, one who prepares and executes training, or one of the crowd who accepts mediocrity as the standard? It's your choice.

What is the first thing I should do with my new platoon?

An associated question would be, "What do my Soldiers expect from me?" The answers to both of these questions are not discovered in any book because each leadership situation requires an assessment by the leader before he acts. However, when a new platoon leader shows up in a platoon, the troops ask the same basic questions:

1. What are the lieutenant's expectations and priorities?

2. Does he have high or low standards?

If you believe the most important job task for your platoon is accurate missile firing procedures, then make sure they understand it. If the platoon is weak in missile reload, then tell them. But also tell them the standards you expect them to attain and how you expect them to reach and maintain those standards. For example, if the Army standard for missile reload is 20 minutes, but you want them to attain 18 minutes, then make your crews attain 18 minutes. You have the authority to raise the Army standard but never lower it. Do not—I repeat, do not—raise an Army standard unless you provide your Soldiers the opportunity to practice that task on a regular basis.

Lieutenant, you are in charge. The Soldiers expect their lieutenant to take charge. However, they do not expect perfection from you, just sincere effort and concern. Soldiers are extremely forgiving when it comes to mistakes as long as they believe the lieutenant is working for and with them. So the answer to both these questions comes down to three words: **be in charge**.

Should I trust my subordinate leaders and Soldiers?

A little philosophy here that some people may not fully agree with, but this is my book, so I'll give you my thoughts. Trust begets trust. I believe that you might find that saying in the Bible. But even if it isn't, it should be. Treat your Soldiers with respect and dignity. Most of them are outstanding men and women who will go out of their way to please you. Let me digress a moment to tell you a personal story from my captain days.

As a new captain arrival in a stateside heavy division ADA battalion, I was granted the opportunity to take command of the "best" battery in the battalion. The commander, a West Point graduate, had taken the unit and improved its record considerably during his command tour. However, I noticed that the morale in the battery wasn't as good as I would expect given the unit's record. It became very apparent to me where the problem lay when I observed a battery formation. The first sergeant, a tough, no-nonsense individual, addressed his Soldiers with the word "dogs." Almost everything that came out of his mouth was of a condescending nature. I expected better from the battery commander but his favorite nickname for his Soldiers was "dirtbags."

A blind man could see that the battery personnel performed their duties more out of fear than out of a sense of personal and unit discipline. Don't get me wrong, I'm all for high standards, but denigration does not equal high standards. I'll say this again because it's important: **denigration does not equal high standards.**

So how does this story relate to the original question? The answer is that trust and respect go hand in hand. If you want respect from your Soldiers, trust and respect them. Let me tell you what this doesn't mean.

It doesn't mean that you skip inspections as I discussed in an earlier question. The Soldiers expect and want you to inspect. How else will they learn your standards? How else will you find those few weaker Soldiers in your platoon? What other tool is more effective in pointing out your priorities to the troops? What about the squad leader or Soldier who fails to meet the standard or breaks that basic trust with you? Denigration is not the solution. Instead, conduct highly visible additional training.

How do I counsel a Soldier?

A good question that needs addressing, but my experience has shown me that the problem with lieutenants and counseling is not the "how" as much as the "when". They are simply afraid to sit down with a subordinate and tell them the positive and negative aspects of his duty performance. I know this is somewhat fundamental, but think back to your high school sport days. How did you improve in your favorite sport? Without a doubt, most of you will say a coach pointed out the good and bad aspects of your play and drove you to work on your weak areas during practice. Well, being a platoon leader parallels this situation. Your subordinates must work together as a team to accomplish your assigned wartime tasks in a proficient and safe manner. You are the head coach of your platoon team, and you are responsible for all aspects of their performance. Your assistant coaches (the squad leaders and platoon sergeant) are present to provide both technical and leader coaching. Hold them responsible for their duties, including counseling of their subordinates.

But how does one actually counsel a Soldier? The answer to this question will vary with your personality, but I would advise that you should first find a quiet place away from the telephone to avoid interruption. Then sit down with your Soldier, most likely with one of your NCOs, and tell them this is a counseling session. Have the Department of the Army-approved counseling form available and write down your comments. Relax and first relate to the Soldier the positive aspects of his performance. Provide him with a positive stroke to start the session. This will relax him and send the message that you observe both sides of his performance. Then insist that he continue the high standards on these tasks. Next lay out for him those tasks or areas that you feel need improvement. Let the discussion be two-way so that the Soldier contributes to the solution. End the session with an agreement or contract of future training events or activities the Soldier will use to improve his performance. Do not let him leave until you summarize the counseling session on the form, then make him sign it. Maintain that form in your personal files for future reference and provide the Soldier a copy. Lastly, I recommend you counsel your subordinate leaders on a monthly basis. Even if a Soldier is performing well, counsel him. It's a great way to praise a subordinate. Who doesn't like to hear praise?

What is the difference between discipline and punishment?

One of the greatest misconceptions by many young lieutenants is that discipline and punishment are one and the same. Nothing could be further from the truth. You can look up the definition in the dictionary and find several meanings. My definition of discipline relating to platoon behavior is that a platoon, first as an organization, then as individuals, will accomplish peacetime and wartime tasks to the proper standard in the absence of the platoon leader. I can define it in a different way for you. The platoon accomplishes the mission in the proper manner because it is the right thing to do.

I understand "on the spot" corrections, but they make me uncomfortable. What is the best way to accomplish them?

It's not unusual for a young lieutenant to feel uncomfortable about correcting an individual "on the spot." Don't worry about the butterflies—they're normal. What is important is that you actually correct the individual or situation. By acting you are reinforcing your own personal high standards.

Think about the message you send your platoon when you don't correct immediately upon finding a deficiency. If the lieutenant doesn't care about the smaller things, then maybe he'll slack off on standards relating to the important wartime tasks.

Remember what I said earlier about platoon discipline in the preceding paragraph? The bottom line is that "on the spot" corrections reinforce unit discipline. So think about what I've told you when you get lazy and don't wish to bother correcting someone. Soldiers understand the idea surrounding "on the spot" corrections, so relax. Most deficiencies in this category are usually simple oversights on the Soldier's part. Just go to the Soldier and point out the deficiency, then ask him if he understands the standard. For example, you observe a five-ton truck carrying Soldiers in the rear cargo area, and realize the safety strap is unsecured. This is obviously an unsafe situation and, as a leader, you must take immediate action to correct the deficiency. It would be proper to stop the vehicle and calmly point out the problem to the driver. Make sure he understands why the safety strap should be secure. Then make him secure it. Don't make him feel like a criminal. Just be insistent that safety standards have been present for a long time and the Army has lost too many Soldiers to injury and death in the past for such a simple safety violation. Don't wait until you experience a soldier death in your unit to become a believer. These corrections save lives.

I can't help throwing in a personal story relating to a failed "on the spot" correction that ended in a Soldier's death. While S3 of an air defense battalion, I was observing a Vulcan firing range. Firing proficiency suffered because of equipment malfunctions resulting in vehicles moving back and forth from garrison to pick up parts. SSG Jones†, a Vulcan mechanic, and SGT Smith†, a Vulcan gunner, were preparing to leave in a HMMWV via a gravel training road toward garrison to pick up some parts and test equipment. Before leaving the area, SSG Jones dutifully placed his helmet on and fastened his seat belt. However, SGT Smith, as the driver, took his helmet off because it was getting heavy and also failed to fasten his seat belt. SSG Jones noted the deficiency, but failed to correct him. It was an extremely dry period and vehicles

† Fictitious name

kicked up dust traversing the road. It so happened that a convoy of five-ton ammunition trucks moving in the opposite direction of the NCOs created a large dust trail. SGT Smith lost his orientation in the dust and had a head-on collision with a large heavily loaded truck. In this case of inadvertent "chicken," the HMMVW lost. SGT Smith's head rocketed into the windshield as the steering wheel, driven forward by the impact, crushed his chest. SGT Smith died within 48 hours. SSG Jones suffered a separated elbow and a few lacerations. He was back to work in a matter of days.

Of course, the loss of SGT Smith was tragic. But to add to the tragedy, about a year later, SSG Jones came up for reenlistment, but decided to leave the U.S. Army. Given that SSG Jones had served for over 10 years of service and was, in my estimation, an overall good Soldier, I decided to talk to him about his decision to leave the U.S. Army. He stated that he just couldn't forgive himself for the *death* of SGT Smith. In his mind, if he had made SGT Smith put his helmet on and buckle his seat belt, he probably would be alive today. The sad truth is that SSG Jones was correct.

Lieutenant, if you correct "on the spot," your Soldiers will too. Your actions will promote a platoon environment that focuses on both excellence and safety.

In the area of military courtesy, what are the minimums I should expect from my Soldiers?

The easy answer to this question is demand the Army standard. But what is the Army standard? Frankly, I don't know, but I know my standard. Below you'll find my pet peeves on this subject:

1. Ensure your troops address you by your rank or Sir. The reason for this is somewhat basic. You're a commissioned officer and your rank demands a certain amount of respect. Personal respect is earned.

2. On the subject of saluting, the Army expects a Soldier to salute when he's about six paces from you. Personally, I expect a little

higher standard in some cases and lower in others. I expect that any Soldier should salute an officer when he executes eye-to-eye contact. This situation may occur at greater than six paces or less. It's just a fundamental recognition of rank that has nothing to do with personality. On the other end of the spectrum, I believe it behooves a platoon leader to designate certain work areas as a platoon non-salute area. The platoon motor pool line might be a good example, for it's extremely awkward for the troops to constantly salute you while they're working on the equipment. I would, however, require saluting on the motor pool line when you conduct your formal platoon inspections.

3. Expect the same military courtesy from the troops for your NCOs as you do for yourself. Your NCOs are hard working junior leaders. The key word here is leaders. They deserve the respect their position enjoys.

My last idiom relating to this topic addresses your conduct rather than the Soldiers:

4. Treat the Soldiers with the same respect and courtesy that you wish them to treat you and your NCOs. The old cliché is true: if you want respect, you must first give respect. Many young lieutenants mistakenly think their subordinates serve them rather than the other way around. Don't fall into that trap.

When one of my Soldiers is having a financial or other related family problem, how should I handle it?

This is one area where a number of leaders will disagree with what I'm about to tell you. In my experience, officers, in general, address Soldiers' family-related problems poorly. I'm not talking about a glitch in the Army system that causes a problem. For example, if finance makes an error relating to the Soldier's pay and he requires assistance, officers can certainly address this systemic problem. But if the issue is domestic violence, alcoholism or other related problems, officers are out of their league. It is best to allow the NCO chain of command to address these types of issues with your backing. You back the NCOs by counseling the Soldier in writing as often as necessary to ensure he understands the proper standard or behavior. I do not recommend that you try to personally act as an arbitrator in a Soldier's family. NCOs and professional counselors are better prepared to handle these situations and you keep yourself out of a potentially compromising position. No matter what you may have been told in the past, the U.S. Army is not primarily a social institution for this country. Its mission is to fight wars and win them. When a Soldier's personal life becomes unmanageable, you have the responsibility to assist him in correcting his problems. However, if he fails to correct the problems, you have a responsibility to eliminate that Soldier from active service. This is not an easy decision for most young lieutenants. But one that you must make.

To illustrate, allow me to tell you a true, but sad story. Years ago when I was a battery commander in an overseas unit, my motor sergeant was very proficient in his job, but had a drinking problem and was 50 pounds overweight. These two character flaws were hurting his performance and overall unit morale. With 17 years of service and the father of four children, I wanted to redeem this NCO if at all possible. I placed him in the hospital for 10 days so that medical professionals could help him address both issues. He continued outpatient care for 6 months, but he had not significantly improved. At this point I placed him in the hospital a second time. Again, he continued to work with medical personnel on an outpatient basis. The NCO chain of command engaged and tried in every manner to assist. However, after a second 6 month period, he again had not shown any improvement in his drinking nor had he lost any real weight. At the 18 year service mark, his reenlistment came due. He was not allowed to reenlist nor reap the benefits of retiring at 20 years.

In retrospect, this NCO, his family, and the US Army would have been better served if his problems had been addressed earlier in his life. As a young NCO, senior NCOs and lieutenants allowed this motor sergeant to scrape by. Behavior problems of this nature are always more successfully addressed earlier rather than later. Lieutenant, you and your NCO chain of command can and do make a difference in people's lives. Do the hard right things and the benefits will be felt not only in your unit, but by families throughout the community.

What is the difference between extra training and extra duty?

A fair question! Many young officers confuse extra training with extra duty. But the former is corrective action designed to help a Soldier reach training standards while the latter is a punitive action. Extra training is like keeping a football team on the practice field until they perfect a new play. Extra duty is like making a football player run extra laps for breaking training rules. It's an important judicial distinction. Don't assume NCOs always follow the book. Don't allow a well meaning NCO to correct a Soldier's behavior with the wrong tool and, in essence, put you in an untenable position. To be more precise, extra duty is punishment in the judicial and non-judicial system. The judicial system addresses Soldier misbehavior via a count martial. The non-judicial system also addresses Soldier misbehavior, but only against minor offenses. The commander administers the non-judicial punishment like extra duty. You, as a lieutenant, cannot direct extra duty for a Soldier, but you may ask for either judicial or non-judicial action against a Soldier to address any misbehavior.

You or your subordinate chain of command may direct a Soldier to participate in extra training. There are several key parts relating to extra training. First, extra training is supervised. Secondly, it must relate to some training deficiency. For example, if your Soldier is deficient at weapons firing, you may not require him to perform extra training that involves digging ditches. In this example, the training must be weapons related.

CHAPTER TWO

So you want to be a Company Commander

As a young battery commander in my first command, I remember cursing the Officer Education System for failing to provide me the background necessary to address the everyday issues that battery commanders face. Yes, the Officer Basic and Advanced Courses gave me an understanding of organizations and capabilities, but not the nitty-gritty detail of what command actually entails. In that first command, I constantly found myself learning many lessons the hard way, impacting not only on unit readiness but on the career progression of some of my Soldiers. However, in my captain days, the average captain had more than one opportunity to command and ultimately save his career. So on my second command, I believe that I finally got the art of command right. But at what price?

Today, young captains receive one chance to command and their career lives or dies with that one shot. Where in the educational system does the average captain attain the working knowledge necessary to provide him the maximum opportunity to succeed? Some senior officers will answer that question by saying that field units have the responsibility to grow future commanders by allowing the lieutenants to progress from one leader position to another. Yes, this is the ***ideal*** *situation, but reality is significantly less grand. Many lieutenants never see the executive officer position or battalion staff before pinning on captain's bars. These less fortunate officers are the ones I hope to assist in this chapter. Just as in the lieutenant chapter, I don't expect you to always agree with my recommendations, but a little forethought on how you would best handle the challenge will go a long way toward ensuring a successful battery/company command tour. Good Luck!*

—FJC

What are the most important aspects of taking command?

The average captain preparing to take his first company command is teeming with anticipation and anxiety. Captain, this is a normal reaction. Don't worry about it, but there are a few things that I wish you would consider before taking control of the guidon. You have only one chance to command and influence a group of men under your tutelage. Nothing is more important than your command responsibilities for the approximate 18 months of a command tour. I'm sure you're asking, "More important than my family?" Of course not, but the family will have to understand that for routine family matters, they will have to take up more of the burden. That means your spouse will have more than her share of family responsibilities. You must impress upon her that your command takes precedence over optional family requirements. For example, instead of going to a movie on a Friday night, you may find yourself in the office writing efficiency reports or award recommendations. That goes with the territory, and the last thing you need is someone pulling you away from responsibilities that you know in your heart need to be done. Now, I'm not saying you should go overboard and ignore your family. You need them, and you can apply the balance and perspective they provide to every individual. Just use good judgment and have your priorities in place.

The second but more important aspect of your command relates to aggressiveness. If you read the lieutenant chapter, you'll remember that I told lieutenants that <u>will</u> is much more important than talent. This statement is doubly true for the young company commander. Time and again I've seen a young, talented commander who, after a few months of command, loses the will to complete the task. This officer has lost perspective of what he is trying to accomplish and is snarled in minutia that he has no business entering into. I have a personal story that illustrates this point.

During my second command tour at Fort Hood, my battalion underwent its yearly unannounced deployment readiness exercise. The evaluation team directed the S3 to prepare a set number of vehicles for full air and rail deployment. Usually, the number of vehicles requested equaled about one battery's worth, so the S3 would split the requirements among the five battery commanders. For this particular exercise, he directed D Battery (my unit) to prepare 13 vehicles; C Battery, 12 vehicles; A Battery, eight vehicles; Headquarters Battery, five vehicles; and B Battery, two vehicles. The S3 based his decision on recent training activities and his best assessment for success. His directions and assessment could not have been more correct. When it was near time for the evaluators to inspect the equipment, A, C, and D Batteries stood tall. Headquarters Battery needed probably another 15 minutes, while B Battery had not even completed one of its five-ton trucks.

Frankly, I couldn't understand the problem. B Battery needed to prepare only two vehicles. I asked myself, "How could B Battery not be ready?" The answer became obvious when I walked over to the B Battery motor line and found the battery commander in a five-ton truck bed with a pair of pliers tightening down the stabilizer wires. Standing alongside the five-ton truck were several outstanding NCOs and Soldiers who looked both disgusted and dumbfounded. It was obvious to a blind man that the battery commander, who wanted to perform well, had lost sight of his position and mission. His mission was to ensure his *unit* performed the test or requirement. I took this young commander aside and tried to explain his role to him, but to no avail. In the end, B Battery failed their portion of the deployment exercise. I wish I could tell you that the B Battery commander learned his lesson and changed. The B Battery commander concluded that he hadn't tried hard enough and on subsequent exercises drove himself into the ground achieving mediocre results at best. He became what I call the "fire hose" type of commander, one who reacts to the current situation and metaphorically puts out fires from day to day. Planning plays a small role in his activities. In the end, this officer type loses his drive because he is always operating from behind compared to his fellow commanders who delegate and plan. Deservedly rated the worst commander in the unit, he lost, first, his perspective of what his role and mission as a battery commander really entailed and, secondly, he ultimately lost his will to perform.

What should be my first decrees as a company commander?

This is a subject area that relates directly to your leadership style, but I believe there are a few minimums that warrant discussion. First, during your change of command ceremony, make sure you tell your troops that you're honored to have the opportunity to *serve them* as their company commander. I didn't make a mistake. I did say you serve your Soldiers. There are too many young officers in the world who become power hungry, who treat their Soldiers with disrespect. Don't you dare become one of them. Your opportunity to command is a once in a lifetime happening that requires a proper perspective. If you serve your Soldiers they will perform their mission, resulting in high unit morale and readiness. Do everything in your power to make your subordinates successful both individually and as a team. To attain these results requires the proper thought process by a company commander.

After the change of command ceremony, form the troops up in some large room and again tell them in so many words how lucky you are to have the opportunity to serve an outstanding group of Soldiers. Excuse the junior enlisted Soldiers so that you will have only leaders remain present. Then explain to the leaders in simple terms your expectations. This should not be a long dissertation. Be direct and forceful, but upbeat. I'll give you my personal expectation speech:

> *"Men, as your new commander, I wish you to know that I only have two expectations. I know that isn't many, so you should pay attention to what I'm talking about.*
>
> *Expectation 1: Perform to the best of your ability. This may seem a bit simplistic to you, but I mean what I say. In every action or requirement that you have, be it exciting or mundane, I expect you to give it your best shot. I've found in my experience that if you perform to the best of your ability on requirements, you will succeed much more often than you fail. Yes, I mean fail. Even the best Soldiers fail every now and then. You will not have any difficulty with me when you fail if I believe you gave me your*

best effort. However, if you can't look yourself in the mirror and tell yourself that you did your best, I will know. Frankly, I'm direct to a fault and I will remind you myself.

Expectation 2: Do not lie, cheat, steal or do anything that discredits you, this unit or the U.S. Army, because no matter how good a Soldier you are, you will pay a heavy price. For example, as leaders you should set the standard for your young Soldiers. We tell them to use their heads when it comes to drinking and driving. If one of you drink and drive, expect a heavy toll both monetarily and career wise. For my leaders, standards are extremely high."

Many senior officers would use a different approach than I, and they would also be correct. The key to your success lies in a little forethought and knowing our strengths and weaknesses. It's important that your approach be authentic and yours alone.

What is the right way to mentor my lieutenants?

Mentorship has as many approaches as it does leader personalities, so there are many ways for you to get this requirement right. In my experience, the issue generally has been not *how* a company commander mentors lieutenants as much as if he mentors them at all. All company commanders, due to their position, are de facto mentors whether they like it or not. Since you have to do it, you might as well do it right.

Let me start with my recommended approach to answer the "how" by asking you a question. When you were a young lieutenant, how did you best learn from your company commander? If you had a good one, I bet you learned by watching him. It's basic human nature that we learn by observing others. So the first thing you must understand is that your lieutenants are watching everything you do, and will generally imitate you to please you. Be conscious of how you react in a given circumstance. Perceptions are truth to young lieutenants.

Of the formal aspect in mentoring, I would recommend that you sit down with each of your lieutenants and discuss their individual and platoon goals. The battalion usually has an officer development program that outlines the preferred skills a lieutenant should attain while in the battalion. Use the officer development program as the starting point in your discussion. Develop a joint assessment of the lieutenant's strengths and weaknesses, then program schools or training time to address the weaknesses. Remember people only learn something when they are required to execute it. Provide them an opportunity; i.e., time to learn a skill. Never lose sight of this. Didn't it take you a few months and training sessions as a young lieutenant to feel comfortable? What leadership and training environment was particularly effective?

The process doesn't end when you've provided the lieutenant with opportunity and time. Every lieutenant requires checking and encouragement. When the lieutenant is training his platoon, give him some time to work with them, and then go out to informally inspect. Provide the lieutenant an opportunity to either shine or fail for you. If the lieutenant is a fast learner and looks good, count your blessings, then praise his efforts. Praise him a second time for good measure. If the lieutenant learns at a steady pace, and most do, ask him what he is doing right and wrong. After an in-depth discussion, and once he understands what needs improving, make him correct the training immediately if possible. Don't forget to praise those small successes in his performance. You may need to stay late in the field or the office, but the rewards you recoup in lieutenant and platoon development and training are worth it.

After about a year most lieutenants become fairly proficient in their duties. Does the mentorship process end? The answer is an emphatic NO. You start the process all over again after placing the lieutenant in a new position. In a normal three-year tour, I would try to provide a lieutenant with the opportunity to be a platoon leader for at least 15 months, followed by 15 months as a company executive officer and a final six months on the battalion staff. Assistant operations officer, if available, is my preferred staff position for lieutenants.

Commanders come and go and their effect on the unit is normally limited to their command tour. But their impact on the young lieutenants serving with them will last a lifetime, be it good or bad. Captain, the manner in which you train and mentor your lieutenants is the long-term measure of your command success or failure. Take this task seriously.

Allow me to illustrate. When I was a battery commander in the 1st Cavalry Division at Fort Hood, Texas, my Battalion Commander walked into my office at the end of a very long day and closed the door. He looked saddened while sitting down in the chair across from my desk. After inviting me to sit, he said, "Captain, I need your help."

"What can I do for you Sir?"

"I'm befuddled. Lieutenant Smith†, the XO at B Battery is failing." He scratched his head and continued, "Smith is a West Pointer who graduated near the top of his class. He's not performing and the only thing he can talk about is getting out of the Army." The battalion commander leaned back in his chair and wiped the perspiration from his hands on his thighs.

"Smith is too talented to lose. I want to put Smith in your battery. Specifically, I want to swap your exec with Smith.

At first, my internal reaction was one of unfairness. I had just fully trained my executive officer over the past 10 months and things were starting to hum in the unit. Taking on a new XO who was failing at another unit was not my idea of a reward for the recent outstanding results the battery had attained. However, I immediately came to my senses and recognized that the Battalion Commander was doing the same thing with this lieutenant that I had done before with a number of NCOs.

I breathed out and said, "Sir, when did you want to make the change?"

Lieutenant Smith was a tremendous talent, however, he was misguided and misused. I loaded up the Lieutenant with heavy responsibilities and monitored each and every one closely at first. As he began to attain results I loosened the reins some and he began to move faster and

---

† Fictitious name

more efficiently. In less than 3 months he proved to be more proficient and talented than my former exec. His growth accelerated so fast over the next 12 months the battalion commander eventually decided to appoint him as my replacement. What a difference a year and leadership efforts make. I'm happy to report that Lieutenant and eventual Captain Smith completed his battery command in a highly successful manner. Unfortunately, he did leave the military several years later. Five years later I ran into Lieutenant Smith at Fort Bliss and learned he had recently been promoted as a Vice President at one of the most prestigious technology firms in the nation.

The key take away from this section is that as a company commander you will have life changing influence on the young officers under your command. True success of your command will be measured by the quality of those leaders who contribute to the US Army mission after you leave the unit.

How do I interact with the battalion commander and gain his confidence?

You gain a battalion commander's confidence first by understanding his priorities and generally attaining them in your unit. Then you make him feel his assistance is unnecessary when addressing a deficiency in your unit. I'll talk about each of these points in a little more depth.

The first requirement to gain the battalion commander's favor is so basic I find it hard to believe some officers do not understand it, but my experience has shown me that many commanders fail in this area. When I was assigned to the 101st Airborne Division (Air Assault), my battalion commander expected each battery commander to strive for 100 percent air assault qualification in the unit. We were in an air assault division, so his expectations made good sense. Some battery commanders were aggressive in attaining school slots and preparing backup Soldiers for last-minute school drops. At least one battery commander would always take a less aggressive attitude and subsequently received fewer school slots. Over time, that battery's air assault qualification rate was significantly less than those with aggressive battery commanders. If you were the battalion commander, wouldn't you wonder about the battery commander who always had the lower qualification rate?

In addressing deficiencies in your unit, make the battalion commander feel that you have the deficiency under control. Provide him with a correction plan, and then see it through. He will be more apt to leave you to your own efforts in the future with little interruption and guidance. On the other end of the spectrum, a great way to lose the battalion commander's confidence is to tell him you will handle something and not follow through.

Battalion commanders come in all personality types. As such, you might have difficulty understanding your battalion commander's true priorities; the Army has a great tool to help you: the Officer Efficiency Report (OER) support form (67-8-1). I highly recommend you fill your form out within your initial 30 days and talk to your battalion commander about it. Failure to complete your OER support form results in a disservice to both you and your battalion commander.

I've provided you with my recommendations on how to gain the battalion commander's confidence, but what is the best way and best time to interact with him? First, don't hide from the battalion commander when he's in your company. Lead him through your area and show him the good things your unit is accomplishing. Address any deficiencies and the corrective actions you are taking in a straight forward manner. Make him feel that you are *in charge* of the company. Not everything is perfect, but assure him that you are taking the necessary steps to correct any problems. It is important you never BS the boss. It will only take one lie to break the important aspect of the relationship—trust.

The last part of the interaction process involves information. Keep the boss informed! Your unit tackles many concurrent daily missions related to personnel, training and support. Brief the battalion commander at least every other day on your activities. You don't need to provide great details. You only provide enough information to show you have things under control.

However, there are some things that happen that are beyond your control. For these types of items no boss likes surprises. For example, if you just learned that one of your troops had been picked up for DUI while he was on leave back home, investigate the incident and then talk to boss as soon as you can. I preferred to walk to battalion headquarters after normal duty hours to chat with the battalion commander on an informal basis. At the same time, I found it prudent to check in with the battalion executive and operations officers. Many times the XO or S3 would provide me with either advice or useful information that helped me handle the immediate or future situations. I can't tell you the time I had saved compared to other battery commanders, because of my informal updates to both the battalion commander and staff. I highly recommend the same technique.

How should I conduct my change of command inventory?

In my early years as a company grade officer, property accountability received little emphasis. Surprisingly, loss of equipment by a company commander was perceived more as a monetary issue than a leadership issue. In the early 1980s, the U.S. Army did an about-face and started to dock outgoing company commanders on their OERs when a large report of survey came out of the command change. My two commands provide a perfect example. After inventorying my first battery, the outgoing commander dealt with a $75,000 (today's dollars) report of survey. Sounds a little high, doesn't it? However, that outgoing commander left the unit with a good OER and an award. The leadership at the time wasn't overly concerned. At the end of my second command three years later, I happened to be leaving at the same time as the Alpha Battery commander. This commander and I were extremely close in tactical and leadership ability. I had great respect for him and his unit in an operating environment. My change of command inventory required me to account for less than $200.00 of lost TA-50. My fellow battery commander had not maintained his hand receipts as well, and his loss of property estimated in the many thousands. When it came to rating time, I had a decided advantage over my fellow battery commander. Our senior rater, the assistant division commander, had respect for the both of us, but he rated only one in the top block. So the important lesson for you on this subject is to maintain property accountability. It's the last thing your rater and senior rater will assess before writing your "command" efficiency report.

Addressing the main question, the key to any change-of-command inventory is preparation. Spend time in the supply room to acquaint yourself with the master automated hand receipt. Check the hand receipt to understand all the items authorized and on-hand in the company. In many cases, substitute items are in place. For example, you may be authorized five-ton trucks, but you may have two-and-a-half-ton trucks in lieu of the authorization. There will be a number of items on the hand receipt you've never seen or heard of before. That's OK, just ask for the manual related to that piece of equipment to ensure you know what it looks like and what it includes. Also look for the shortage annexes to major items so you don't sign for the entire piece unknowingly. An example might be the average wrecker, which consists of a five-ton truck and crane with a full complement of ancillary equipment. The truck might be missing the blow torch mechanism. The shortage annex should have a record of the missing item.

Once you've fully acquainted yourself with the automated hand receipt, check the present commander's sub-hand receipts. Validate that all items on the automated hand receipt are accounted for in the company's sub-hand receipts. I understand this is a painstakingly slow task, but it needs to be done in a meticulous manner. How else can you be sure? Generally you will find some discrepancies. Just have the supply sergeant make the corrections as part of the updated hand receipt.

Only after you've completed this slow task should you start inventorying the company. Schedule the inventories, in advance, on the training schedule. They are too important to conflict with other training events. I recommend that you allocate about three hours for each major hand receipt, but this time may vary depending on the items to be inventoried. For example, your tool room will take an afternoon to inventory, while an arms room will probably only take about two hours. Your supply sergeant can provide a good estimate as to how much time each hand receipt requires to complete.

When you schedule the inventories, it's important that you inventory like hand receipts on the same day. For example, all weapon systems platoons who generally have the same equipment should lay out their equipment on the same day. You must prevent the platoons from exchanging equipment for the inventory. Trust me. It will happen, not only between platoons but also between companies. As an incoming battery commander at Fort hood, I found out that the two swim kits in my battery were also being carried on the hand receipt of my neighbor commander. After probing with my fellow battery commander, we found that there were four swim kits at one time, but two had been turned in. The neighbor unit had not been given a turn-in credit. As a result, several platoon sergeants of the two different batteries agreed to cover each other in the event of an inspection or inventory.

Once you complete the company inventory, account for all discrepancies before you take command. Do not accept a promise from the outgoing company commander that he will correct a problem later. When you sign your name on that automated hand receipt, those problems belong to you. So demand that the outgoing company commander find the property, pay for it himself, or initiate a report of survey. In any case, be up-front with the battalion executive officer and commander about your findings. Your allegiance is not to the outgoing commander, but to the senior leadership in the battalion.

What should be my priorities as a commander?

You're probably saying, what a dumb question. Everyone knows that the company commander's priorities are the same as the battalion commander's. Well, that's true and not true. Your long-range priorities certainly should coincide, but your short-range ones may not be exactly the same. The Army's training management system requires you to assess the strengths and weaknesses of your unit. You must train those tasks upon those your unit requires improvement or sustainment, as the case may be. My point is that you are the commander, and you have the leeway to decide what's best for your unit as long as you work within the framework of the battalion commander's policies, guidance and standards. I always tell young commanders to trust their instincts. Ninety-nine percent of the time they are right. Here's a personal example to illustrate my point.

My second battalion commander was a stickler on weapon system crew drills. I understood this and made them a priority in my training plan. The battalion was scheduled to undergo a division IG inspection two weeks hence and I felt uncomfortable about a number of areas in the battery, so I went to the battalion commander to request permission to change my training schedule from crew drills to IG preparation. I felt that my crews were the best in the battalion and the time would be better served performing other tasks. In the end, the battalion commander allowed me to stand down one platoon at a time to address IG deficiencies while the other platoons maintained their normal schedule. The battalion commander's solution was actually more efficient than mine, for the unit was able to pass the IG inspection and maintain proficient crews at the same time.

Good company commanders know what's best for their unit and are not afraid to fight for what they believe is best for all concerned. They also know that in the absence of guidance, their priorities should support, in some way, the unit's wartime mission.

What items should I maintain in my company commander's notebook?

Let me answer this question by using as a basis my recommendations to the lieutenants in an earlier chapter. If lieutenants have the below information in their notebook, what does a company commander need in addition?

Notebook information

Troop Information

Name

MOS, rank, date of rank

Date eligible for next promotion

Civil school level

Marital status, number of dependents and names

Required schooling (military and civilian, i.e. GED)

Home address and phone number, if applicable

Reenlistment eligibility date

Platoon Items

Mission statement

Platoon collective tasks

Battle crews

Equipment status

OPD checklist

Key phone numbers

Personnel accountability roster

I recommend that a company commander also include the items listed below

Command-Specific Items

Master training plan

Quarterly training guidance

6 weeks of training schedules

Company reenlistment goals and eligible's

30-60-90 day personnel losses

Critical personnel shortages

Incoming personnel list with sponsors names

Consolidated 2406, Equipment Status

Requisition numbers and line items for major supply shortages

Work order status-station property (barracks, etc.)

OPD checklist for each of your lieutenants

Sound like a lot of unnecessary garbage to you? It is far from it. If you are paying attention to the listed areas on a regular basis, few mission requirements will go untouched. Of all the things a company commander must manage, the one thing the average commander has problems with is time. An organized company commander uses the time available to accomplish tasks concurrently in many areas of his company. Your company commander notebook will help you focus on the most important unit activities and assist you in accomplishing more with less time.

What is the best way to use my executive officer (XO)?

I suggest that there are two schools of thought on this subject. One suggests that the XO is just like another platoon leader who happens to have administration requirements and that you treat him the same as the other lieutenants. The other school of thought elevates the power of the XO by using him more as a deputy commander with the authority to push lieutenants to get things done. I fall more in the second school of thought and there is a good reason for this. Let me explain.

As a company commander, you are ordained by your position a certain power base. You have the option to maintain the power within you or share that power with your subordinates. I believe that as a general rule you should share that power. For when you do, your power base actually grows—you enhance your ability to influence the farthest appendages of your organization. You do not, however, want to share that power with someone you don't trust, and this situation does occur on occasion.

Specifically, I would task the XO to be the honest broker on all the support areas for both the garrison and in the field. For example, I would give the XO the authority to inspect maintenance in the line platoons whether the company commander is around or not. He would have the authority to order corrective action, including work after duty hours. The line lieutenants are required to comply if they know what is good for them. Of course, the XO is only able to make things happen if the company commander supports his decisions.

The XO is directly responsible for the company command post in the field. I hold him and the first sergeant responsible for its operation and set up. This includes a canned VIP briefing with charts, etc. Lastly, I make the XO my confidante in as many areas as possible so that he understands my thought process and goals. This serves two purposes: it enhances your power base and provides for officer development in the individual. Remember, your XO will probably be aspiring for a command soon after the Officer Advanced course. Provide him with insights to your actions. Allow time for him to ask questions and converse on any subject relating to leadership, unit activities, and personnel actions that helps his personal or unit growth.

How do I maintain and train at the same time?

One of the great mistakes many young company commanders make is to differentiate between training and maintenance. To borrow a saying from the 1st Cavalry Division, "Training is Maintenance and Maintenance is Training." The 1st Cavalry leadership wants you to believe that maintenance is a part of your daily activities. This really makes sense. In the Army, we say we wish to shoot, move and communicate. Maintenance is an integral part of all three aspects of these missions. So make maintenance a part of everything you do. For example, I recommend that prior to any field training exercise you conduct a maintenance inspection. During the exercise you inspect equipment along with the operations. Lastly, inspect unit maintenance again prior to moving back to the motor pool. With this kind of emphasis by the company commander, routine maintenance will actually become routine.

Many company commanders fail in the maintenance arena because they don't understand what maintenance really means. Maintenance is a process, not an event. I've seen a company commander pulled one way and then the other addressing one maintenance problem after another. As a company commander, you must put in place the procedures that ensure a high state of readiness. For example, your PLL is the lifeblood of the maintenance system. Is your PLL clerk trained? What is your zero balance? Are you programming your quarterly, semiannual and annual services on the training calendar? These are the types of maintenance issues the company commander should be addressing. He should not be making special parts runs or putting any type of tool to a weapon system or vehicle.

As a side note, I recommend that you conduct your services as a platoon and place this event on the training schedule. Specifically, have the platoon vehicles inspected prior to the service. On the first day of the service, make the platoon leader lay out all the parts and tools required to finish the service. Provide the platoon leader with a vehicle and system mechanic and hold him responsible for the job. Once the lieutenant indicates he's done, ask the warrant officer in your company or battalion to inspect every vehicle for completeness and thoroughness. Since the lieutenant is being held accountable, the warrant officer is more likely to give you an accurate assessment of the services than if you were to hold him accountable. In my book, good services equal good training and good maintenance.

How much leeway do I give my first sergeant?

The straight answer to this question, without belaboring the point, is as much as possible. What's more important for your command is the communication link between you and the first sergeant. Remember, the first sergeant is an individual with many years of service. He knows how to get things done. That's why it's important that the company commander be the company planner and lay out the goals and missions. The first sergeant is an executor. If the first sergeant has a clear understanding of what you wish to accomplish, he will back you in everything he does. In the absence of clear guidance, he will probably assess, by himself, the overall requirements and get things done. This might unintentionally have the two of you working against one another at times. This situation occurs more often than you might think because of the pressures the first sergeant receives from the command sergeant major. Sometimes you might have to remind the first sergeant that he works for you and not the command sergeant major. If this does occur, I wouldn't look any farther than the mirror for the culprit. You failed to provide proper vision and guidance.

To illustrate my point of miscommunication and lack of guidance, I'll give you a personal example from my battery command days at Fort hood, Texas.

I decided to move my firing platoons out to the field for a two-day exercise, wishing to see them perform critical collective tasks that an outside team would evaluate the following month. I was determined that they would reach my standards or stay in the field until they did. That meant staying in the field beyond the two days if necessary. This was a smart, aggressive and tough approach, except that I failed to tell the first sergeant of my intention to keep the platoons in the field past the programmed two days. He was the one who had arranged to feed the troops hot meals in the field and had done so for the two programmed days. However, when I demanded that the platoons stay in the field, how was I to feed them without prior coordination? The first sergeant ensured the troops were fed on the third day. However, he called in a number of favors to make it happen. Unfortunately, he had to use those favors to cover one of my mistakes. The first sergeant would have handled this ahead of time if I had given him my vision and expectations. Don't make the mistake I did. Always ensure the first sergeant understands your intentions and expectations.

Who wrote my MTOE and how do I get something changed?

The process of TOE (table of organization and equipment) development is somewhat long and complicated, but I'll try to provide a simplified and shortened explanation. Based on doctrine, threat and weapon systems capabilities, a notional fighting unit is designed by the Directorate of Combat Developments at the respective TRADOC combat or support center, with assistance from many sources. The Combined Arms Command at Fort Leavenworth approves the design and then builds a base TOE for this type unit. Once approved by the Department of the Army, the base TOE is used by the major commands to tailor the unit to their specific wartime requirements. Let's use CENTCOM as an example of a major command. CENTCOM headquarters would adjust the base TOE of the unit, generating what is called a modified TOE or MTOE. So to answer the first part of the main question, your major headquarters (CENTCOM, USAREUR, EUSA, etc.) developed your MTOE.

Of course, as modernization occurs, there is a process to update both the base TOE and MTOE. The base TOE is updated semiannually through a U.S. Army Training and Doctrine Command review process that requires Department of the Army approval. You need not concern yourself with this. However, you may want to concern yourself with the MTOE review process that might directly affect your unit. If you have some significant problems with your MTOE, your S3 has the direct responsibility to address it. Through him and the battalion commander you would submit a change to your MTOE to correct the deficiencies. From the S3 the request moves up the operational chain until it reaches the major command headquarters. This is where your change package will be reviewed.

Final approval still lies with Department of the Army, but major command changes are rarely challenged. Even if approved, however, implementing the change will take from six months to a year.

Given the difficulty in making a change to your MTOE, why undertake such a challenge? The answer is simple. You have the power to morph your unit into a more modern and effective fighting unit. You may not ever be the beneficiary of the true impact of your change, but that doesn't matter. What does matter is that your changes add capabilities to the unit that might save Soldiers lives in the future. Isn't that a legacy you could live with?

How do I requisition the right people at the right grade?

You don't, but your battalion S1 does. In fact, your S1 requisitions people based on the needs of the battalion compiled from a list of shortages from every company. So there are several questions that you need to ask the S1 based on your personnel needs. First, ask him what he perceives your greatest needs are for your company. Personnel reports are sometimes made out by the first sergeant, and it's been known for a first sergeant to try and influence his needs rather than yours. So you should ensure that you and the S1 are requisitioning your needs based on your priorities. My experience has shown that low-density MOSs are particularly critical to a company. I've found that capable motor mechanics, communication personnel and a supply sergeant are particularly critical to mission accomplishment.

After clearing up this issue, ask the S1 for his projected inbound personnel listing and his recommended company assignment. From this information, you may ascertain some inequities in what the other company commanders are requesting or receiving. You have the right to your fair share of new personnel entering the battalion. No one really understands your needs or looks out for that share of personnel in the battalion—no one really looks out for that share except you and the first sergeant.

During my battery command time at Fort Hood, I was personally affected by this inequity. The situation developed when a young battery commander, who happened to be well liked by the battalion commander, seemed to be having difficulty accomplishing his mission. This young battery commander complained that he was short experienced leadership in the NCO ranks. To correct the perceived situation, the battalion commander took the best platoon sergeant from each of the other batteries and placed them in this young battery commander's unit. He then force-fed personnel into his unit at the expense of the rest of the battalion. On the surface, the battalion commander's motives seemed shortsighted. He just wanted to save this young battery commander from failure. However, in a relatively short time, the batteries cut off from the personnel stovepipe were in dire need of replacements. When I could no longer, in my estimation, perform my battery mission adequately, I sat down with the battalion commander and S1 and pointed out, line by line, the personnel holes in my unit that required immediate filling. The battalion commander, blinded by his earlier decision, finally woke up to the problem and opened the personnel pipeline. Actually, a few personnel were reallocated to address immediate needs in the bare batteries.

There is a lesson to this story. The young battery commander who was in trouble ended up failing anyway. He generally had the same personnel shortages as other batteries in the battalion but failed to use his assets properly and effectively. At your level I would not recommend this approach to "help" a failing platoon leader. You will do more harm than good. It would be best that you directly address the lieutenant's failure to lead effectively with his current personnel assets.

What is the best way to handle my warrant officers?

The answer to this question relates directly to your overall attitude toward warrant officers. Some commissioned officers believe warrant officers are technical experts. These technical experts address the specific weapon system operational readiness problems above and beyond the normal maintenance. This attitude toward warrant officers was the norm when I was a young lieutenant, but in 1985 a new warrant officer study formally changed the role of the warrant officer. A warrant officer is certainly the technical expert in the battalion, but he is also a leader and trainer. Earlier I told you that maintenance is a process. The main figure in molding the maintenance process in your company (if you have one) is the warrant officer. I would hold him responsible to oversee the second echelon aspect of the program. In this position, he is not only responsible for the system and motor mechanics activities, he is also responsible for maintenance for all activities (communications, NBC, etc.). Charge him with the growth in personnel maintenance skills as well. He has the technical expertise to ensure quality control of the second echelon work.

Use the warrant officer as a technical inspector prior to special exercises or inspections, but try to never use him to fix something. He can certainly help troubleshoot, but if the warrant officer continually has a wrench in his hand, you've lost the maintenance battle in the company.

The warrant officer should work directly for you and be senior rated by either the battalion executive officer or commander. With this control you can imprint your vision and goals directly on the warrant officer. However, I caution you not to hold him directly responsible for deadlined vehicles. That responsibility always stays with the platoon leader. The warrant office will stay to fix the item, but the pressure belongs to the platoon leader. The warrant officer rarely owns a vehicle of his own. He owns the maintenance process.

Usually the warrant officer is the best trainer of maintenance in the company, but do not overuse him in this capacity. Your platoons should not be dependent on him for their maintenance and training. I recommend that you require the warrant officer to personally assist in the platoon leader's personal maintenance training. It's to the warrant officer's advantage in the maintenance process to have highly knowledgeable and skilled platoon leaders. They will save him numerous headaches.

How should I run my company?

What a tough question. The answers vary depending on the type of unit and its mission. However, I believe there are a few common threads in running a company that cut across all weapon systems and units. I'll address this question by giving you my rules for a company commander.

Rule 1: Be in charge. Make decisions and follow through on them. Yes, you will make mistakes on occasion, but it's a worse error to be indecisive. So on a daily basis, reinforce your short-term goals with your subordinates and emphasize your long-term goals on a weekly basis.

Rule 2: Mean what you say and say what you mean. Everything that you do or say has an impact on the company. Make sure that the intended impact is received by the unit. For example, if you harp on maintenance deficiencies, but apply little pressure without repercussions for failure, the troops will learn two things. First, you're not serious about maintenance, and second, you have no bite in your bark. This will result in a drop in company efficiency and discipline. The unit might even fail in its mission at a most critical moment.

Rule 3: Never talk down to junior Soldiers. If things are going awry in your company the culprit lies with your chain of command which is not enforcing your standards. You might need to pull a few leaders aside and get mad at them. Do so if required, but do it away from the troops.

Rule 4: Develop and execute daily, weekly and monthly goals for your company. Be consistent in attaining these goals so the troops understand the real priorities.

Rule 5: Touch every aspect of your unit by visiting or inspecting it once a week. In answering the main question, this is the technique that I recommend. Your company is already broken into smaller organizations, so you can schedule yourself to informally visit an area ahead of time. For example, every Friday evening I would write on my calendar next to each day of the upcoming week which areas, platoons or organizations I would visit. Typically I would check the motor pool areas and platoon equipment on Mondays and Fridays, supply and arms room on Wednesday, and NBC equipment on Thursdays. Training was always checked as it was scheduled while I randomly inspected the barracks except during scheduled command inspections. The key to this technique is your visibility and interest. This technique serves two leadership purposes as well. First, it shows the troops that you're serious about what you say. Secondly, it provides the Soldier an opportunity to talk and show the boss what he is accomplishing. This makes for a more satisfied and informed Soldier.

Rule 6: Do routine things in your company routinely. I once heard this statement from a senior officer and liked it, so I use it. What does this statement mean exactly? It means that on all those daily requirements that every company must face, accomplish them with a high standard as a normal part of the day. For example, police call is required by just about every unit in the Army. Do police call by platoon and make them do it with a high standard. The Charge of Quarters (CQ) is your representative during non-duty hours. Don't you want a professional representative performing his duties properly? I assure you that a company commander who emphasizes standards on routine requirements will grow a highly disciplined unit.

Rule 7: Believe in yourself. If you don't, why should anybody else?

Rule 8: Will is more important than smarts as a commander. History is full of examples of people who will themselves to victory on the battlefield and in life. Never give up, no matter what the circumstances.

I remember a battery commander that impressed me with his will during an externally evaluated Army training and evaluation program. The first requirement for his unit was to conduct a night move over an extended distance. The battery executive officer was leading the battery column at an excessive speed and extended intervals. After traveling on an off-road, dusty trail for about 10 miles, he made a wrong turn at a four-way intersection. Due to the extended interval, groups of vehicles got lost on differing trails for most of the night. This is not the best way to start out an evaluated ARTEP to say the least. However, the battery commander did not panic. He rallied his leaders and Soldiers with his brand of determined leadership. When the morning mission started his unit was in position—a little shaky, but functioning. On each following mission of the four-day ARTEP the battery improved its performance. At the end of the ARTEP, the evaluators noted the improvement and were impressed with the recovery of the unit given the first night's maneuver error. The battery received excellent ratings and I was highly impressed by this battery commander's personal performance. I would go to war anytime with that young man. More importantly, I would trust him to lead my son in battle.

Rule 9: Do most of your paperwork after normal duty hours. This rule helps you in two ways. First, it keeps you out of the office during the most important part of the training day. Secondly, your paperwork is completed in a quieter environment which contributes to a more efficient work period.

What's the right way to give an Article 15?

I think it's appropriate to first discuss general legal issues. It's extremely difficult for a young officer to obtain legal training in preparation for his company command. The situation worsens for the company commander because, in many cases, the battalion commander cannot, per regulation, coach or guide him. So what can a company commander do? Call your local judge advocate general as often as necessary. It's their job to assist commanders. So don't be shy.

To answer the main question, I must first remind you what you represent when giving an Article 15. In essence you wear the hats of the prosecuting attorney, the defense attorney, jury and judge all at the same time. The troops know this and they watch the company commander to sense his fairness, both in judgment and punishment. Article 15's will either enhance or hurt unit discipline. It all depends on the message that the troops perceive. Think about this ahead of time so that you temper and tailor your actions.

In the actual procedure, I recommend that the platoon leader or first sergeant conduct the first reading of the Article 15. Provide the Soldier the opportunity to see a legal assistance officer as required per regulation. When his is ready to see you, schedule the second reading after normal duty hours. Have the entire chain of command present with any potential witnesses required for testimony. The chain of command should first provide you with the evidence against the Soldier while the Soldier is waiting outside. Once the initial testimony is heard, have the Soldier formally report to you. Place him at ease and then explain to him his rights under Article 15. He may wish to go the court martial route and that is his right. Never flinch from allowing him this right, for many a Soldier tries to bluff the commander. If he accepts the Article 15, tell him you have not, as yet, made any judgment and you wish to provide him with the opportunity to present anything in mitigation or extenuation. It's important at this point that you truly listen to the Soldier and any evidence. The chain of command sometimes has a narrow view of the Soldier and it's your job to be more objective.

I caution you not to take a negative attitude toward any Soldier. I've seen battery commanders with a belittling attitude that takes individual dignity away. Even if the Soldier is guilty as sin, allow him to maintain some dignity by addressing his violation and the price that he has to pay for his unacceptable act or behavior. Tell him that once he undergoes punishment, the slate is clean and you want him as a contributing member of your unit.

When addressing the Soldier, always comment in a matter-of-fact manner. You should show as little emotion as possible, even if you personally dislike the individual.

My last point of advice on this issue relates to punishment if you find a Soldier guilty. Like crimes do not necessarily require like punishment. Every case is new and must be judged on its own merits. Seek the counsel of the Soldier's chain of command. Matters of mitigation are important. Do you give the same punishment to a good Soldier who strays versus a historically poor performer? If somebody disagrees with your judgment of a Soldier, and someone always will, you have no obligation to explain why one Soldier's punishment was more severe than another. Just say that every case you adjudge is decided objectively on its own merits.

What are my courses of action to prevent family-related problems?

Some cynics would tell you that man is basically a troublemaker so you cannot prevent problems. I say hogwash. In my experience the average Soldier family problems relate to:

poorly informed spouses;

undisciplined financial management, particularly as it relates to balancing a checkbook;

children or spousal neglect and abuse; and

alcohol abuse by the Soldier

Have no doubt that you will see these types of problems during your command tenure, but I'm convinced that there are commander initiatives that diminish these problems to a more manageable level.

You will be amazed at how little military spouses understand about the Army, your community and unit. There are spouses who haven't the faintest idea what her husband really does for a living. The sad part about this situation is that many immature Soldiers intentionally keep their spouses in the dark. Apparently, it's a form of power that the Soldier lords over the spouse. As commander, you have an obligation to combat this unfortunate circumstance. A regular family day at the unit with you answering questions and providing a briefing solves most of the general information problems, but not the all the problems. Some issues need specific attention by either the NCO chain of command or an informal spouse's network. An informal spouses' chain passes information around via telephone or a monthly newsletter. This aspect is purely voluntary, and not all the spouses will want to take part, but you'll find enough spouses interested that it will be well worth the effort.

Remember when you bounced your first check? I'm sure you were embarrassed and so was I. The inexperienced Soldier and his wife are prime candidates for financial disaster. No one has shown them how to manage a monthly budget. They pay bills as they come and spend money on unnecessary items because they fail to understand what financial management means. You usually do not directly influence a Soldier in financial areas unless he's severely in debt and the creditors are calling you daily. To prevent this debt problem from becoming too severe, insist that the Soldier and spouse seek help from the financial counselor at Army Community Service. Every post maintains an office for just such problems. Through your subordinate chain of command, demand that these services be used. If not, hold the Soldier's chain of command responsible.

Spouse and child abuse demand serious attention by the chain of command. At the first sign of a problem, direct the Soldier and spouse to undergo family counseling. Don't intervene in family affairs, but talk to the counselor directly for advice on what you can do to help. The best you can probably do is provide written counseling to the Soldier on what is and is not acceptable behavior. If the family situation improves with time, give the Soldier positive strokes. If counseling fails, prepare the paperwork to chapter the Soldier out of the Army. Some leaders do not agree with my approach, but I believe that the U.S. Army doesn't need abusive Soldiers no matter how good they are on the job.

Alcohol has always been and will continue to be the Soldier's drug of choice. Yes, you will catch a few using hard drugs; just chapter them out of the Army. But how do you handle cases of alcoholism? I'll start my answer by telling you about a case during my battery command days at Fort Hood.

SSG(P) Hammond† arrived in my unit from Germany as a heralded noncommissioned officer. He certainly looked and talked the role of an outstanding rising star. His selection as a SGT Morales club member reinforced this image. But SSG(P) Hammond's drinking was out of control before he even arrived in my unit. Debt notices started to flow into my office. SSG(P) Hammond failed to report on time at least once per week. His appearance and performance degenerated. I was unaware of his drinking problem, so SSG(P) Hammond's behavior

† Fictitious name

puzzled me until I received a phone call for the AER office to confirm that I signed a loan request for him. They possessed a document with my alleged signature. I had not approved or signed anything, so the document was a forgery. I called SSG(P) Hammond into my office after obtaining a copy of the document to investigate. At this time, the whole truth about his drinking problem came out. After the meeting, the first sergeant and I immediately transported SSG(P) Hammond to the alcohol and drug treatment facility. I wished him to understand that I would stand by him in his battle against this disease. However, within a few days, the battalion commander, per my request, gave SSG(P) Hammond an Article 15. I reduced him to E5 and made him a squad leader. In essence, I made him reach bottom for a man of his military accomplishments.

There is a happy ending to this story. SGT Hammond had a girlfriend who stood by him and together they overcame the alcohol problem and realigned his debt. Months later SGT Hammond was promoted back to SSG. On that same day, he walked into my office and thanked me for saving him. The truth is, he saved himself, for with one more setback I would have chaptered this capable individual out of the Army.

I believe this story illustrates my philosophy on this issue. You can't stop Soldiers from drinking, but you can discourage them. The best way I've found is by demanding the company conduct physical training every day of the week. Also, schedule unit runs immediately following paydays even if it isn't your normal day. Those Soldiers who had too much to drink the night before will fall out of the run, puke and feel awful. On the next payday, they will remember that terrible feeling and most will not partake in too much drink the night of payday.

All company commanders make mistakes, but what are the types of mistakes that are excusable and which ones are not?

Most of the mistakes as a company commander are recoverable. The key point with many senior leaders relates to how well you react and recovery after a mistake. My earlier example of a battery commander recovering his unit after a failed tactical move during an evaluated ARTEP illustrates this point perfectly. Never give up after a mistake. Will is more important than talent.

There are some mistakes that will make you less favored than your fellow company commanders in the battalion. These are the mistakes that embarrass the battalion commander in some way. You've heard the cliché, "Never surprise the boss." It's true. No boss likes to be surprised and embarrassed by something one of his companies failed to accomplish. We all fail in life occasionally and company commanders are no exception. Just don't let your boss be surprised by the event. You be the first one to inform him of the bad news—don't let some outside or higher command break it to him.

Mistakes that involve integrity or character destroy your credibility and career. When you start asking yourself whether it's smart to violate a regulation to look better, you're thinking is wrong. Don't do it. Admit to mistakes and deficiencies and take appropriate corrective action. Perfection is not expected, but outstanding effort and solid character are the minimum requirements of any company commander.

During my days at Fort Hood, a new battery commander lost some test equipment through negligence. Instead of coming forward, he tried to steal the test equipment from another battery. By chance, someone caught him and he was immediately relieved of his duties. DUMB! He could have come forward and the worst that would have happened would have been a verbal reprimand with $200.00 coming out of his pocket. His mistake was recoverable but he chose wrong. So in your decision-making process, understand that a little embarrassment is far better than choosing an improper path.

One other crystal ball that you shouldn't drop relates to safety. Never authorize activity out to the bounds of regulation or safety standards. If you do, serious repercussions will surely follow. Out of an idea of machismo, a general officer in the 1980s authorized Soldiers to parachute when he knew the wind conditions were unsafe. One Soldier died and numerous others were injured. This kind of error is unacceptable and unrecoverable, because it shows a serious lack of judgment. Why should the Army allow this kind of leader to jeopardize its greatest asset, its Soldiers? I certainly would not.

How do I handle the counseling of my lieutenants? Are there any preferred methods?

Think back for a minute to when you were a young platoon leader. Did your company commander counsel you in a manner that provided direction and inspiration? What would you have done differently if you were in his place today? These are the questions you must ask and answer now, before you take that company command. There are no preferred methods to lieutenant counseling, but the most effective method will fit your leadership style and capabilities. Be yourself.

My lieutenant counseling method served me well and it might you as well. First, I used the 67-8-1 OER support form in the initial counseling session. The lieutenant and I both signed the form, representing a contract between us. During the following quarterly counseling sessions, I used two handwritten 67-8 OER forms. One form was written in blue and the other red. The red OER form indicated a direct evaluation of his performance to date. Positive and negative comments provided both strokes and reprimands and eliminated misunderstandings of what the lieutenant did right and wrong during the rated period. The blue OER form was written in formal OER language to illustrate the actual OER rating he would receive if I was to rate him that day. Before the lieutenant left my office he understood his strengths and weaknesses, from my perspective, and what I expected him to accomplish in the upcoming quarter. No matter which method you choose, if the lieutenant understands your standards and goals after a counseling session, you've succeeded in a significant part of your leadership responsibilities.

Of course, you must monitor the lieutenants' performance during the quarter and mark both good and bad efforts in your company commander notebook. When the OER time comes around you are well prepared to write and justify any OER be it outstanding, good, mediocre or poor.

Lastly, understand the OER system so that you may properly serve your lieutenants. Every evaluation has its nuances and its important you understand the US Army's system. I address this topic in the next chapter.

CHAPTER THREE

The Art of OER Painting

A few years ago I heard that IBM Corporation undertook a major study of the Army's officer efficiency report (OER) and promotion system. Apparently they liked how the system promoted merit and they wanted to adapt many of its procedures. I must agree with IBM that our OER promotion system is good, given the failings of human nature. The US Army and any other worthy institution want to promote the most talented and deserving that exhibit the highest standards in personal character. There are, however, a few officers who make rank who don't deserve the honor, while there are deserving officers who fail to receive a promotion. How and why does this situation come about? There are conditions in which the needs of the US Army outweigh the merit review of the officer review board. For example, after the review board has completed their order of merit list, they then match the promotions to the specific needs of the US Army. If the Army happens to need a Chinese Intelligence expert and one was not chosen on the first round, the review board will then go back to find a qualified Chinese Intelligence expert in the initial non-select group. If they find one, the selection board will move that individual to the select list and move down the last name on the merit list. In some cases, personality conflicts play a role play in some officers receiving objective ratings. But in other situations, which is the purpose of this chapter, poor OER writing by the rater and senior rater is at fault. This latter point is what I wish to address in this chapter.

You may be an outstanding company commander yet incur career damage due to an uncaring rater or senior rater. Or you might have an exceptional lieutenant working for you and he receives a thoughtless and undeserving rating. Won't happen to me, you say? Trust me on this point. Some field grade officers fail to spend adequate time and thought in writing OERs. Your command OERs are the most important ones you'll receive as a young officer. Without a successful company command and a properly written command OER, you will not progress to the rank you deserve.

This chapter provides my recommendations to the rater and senior rater as to the proper writing of OERs. When writing OERs for the lieutenants under your command, understand the nuances of the system and give them the ratings they deserve, good or bad. Also, pay attention to the senor rater requirements so that you can lobby with your rater for the proper comments in your and your lieutenants OERs. Don't be bashful with your rater. The stakes are too high for you not to understand the OER system.

—FJC

OER writing, like officership, is an art form. Officers who understand this art form can paint the proper images of their subordinates for a prospective board member. However, officers who do not understand the nuances of the OER system may actually do a disservice to their hardworking, loyal people. This chapter provides my personal tips on accepted norms and how you might stylize your OERs to support the image you wish to project. For brevity purposes, I will concentrate on positive OERs.

Let's begin by outlining the roles and responsibilities of the various players as outlined in the US Army regulation.

Rated Officer Responsibilities

Perform each assigned or implied duty

Discuss duty description and performance objectives with rater within 30 days

Revise and update objectives and duty description

Accurately describe duties, objectives and significant contributions on DA Form 67-9-1 and 67-9-1a at the end of the rating period

Rater Responsibilities

Provide his/her and the senior rater's support forms to the rated officer

Discuss scope of rated officer's duties within 30 days

Counsel rated officer throughout the rating period utilizing the DA Form 67-9-1

Review DA Form 67-9-1 at end of rating period

Verify and enter the rated officer's APFT and height and weight data on DA Form 67-9

Assess and evaluate performance of officer on DA Form 67-9

Senior Rater Responsibilities

60 day minimum

Ensure support form is provided

Become familiar with rated officer's performance

Assess rated officer, considering DA Form 67-9-1 and potential relative to his/her contemporaries

Has rated officer signed the DA Form 67-9?

The first and obvious question is "Is that all?" Is that the sum total of what you can gain from the Army Regulation? Of course not. However, the regulation covers the rules for OERs—when and how they should be submitted, i.e. the circumstances or conditions, etc. This is important for managing the OER system, but not important for the purposes of this book. What is important is how the promotion boards evaluate the respective sections on the OER form. Turn the page and review DA Form 67-9 (Officer Evaluation Report).

OFFICER EVALUATION REPORT
For use of this form, see AR 623-3; the proponent agency is DCS, G-1.

FOR OFFICIAL USE ONLY (FOUO)
SEE PRIVACY ACT STATEMENT IN AR 623-3.

PART I - ADMINISTRATIVE DATA

a. NAME (Last, First, Middle Initial) | b. SSN | c. RANK | d. DATE OF RANK(YYYYMMDD) | e. BRANCH | f. DESIGNATED SPECIALTIES / PMOS (WO)

g. 1. UNIT, ORG., STATION, ZIP CODE OR APO, MAJOR COMMAND | g. 2. STATUS CODE | h. REASON FOR SUBMISSION

i. PERIOD COVERED: FROM (YYYYMMDD) | THRU (YYYYMMDD) | j. RATED MONTHS | k. NONRATED CODES | l. NO. OF ENCL | m. RATED OFFICER'S AKO EMAIL ADDRESS (.gov or mil) | n. UIC | o. CMD CODE | p. PSB CODE

PART II - AUTHENTICATION *(Rated officer's signature verifies officer has seen completed OER Parts I-VII and the admin data is correct)*

a. NAME OF RATER (Last, First, MI) | SSN | RANK | POSITION | SIGNATURE | DATE (YYYYMMDD)

b. NAME OF INTERMEDIATE RATER (Last, First, MI) | SSN | RANK | POSITION | SIGNATURE | DATE (YYYYMMDD)

c. NAME OF SENIOR RATER (Last, First, MI) | SSN | RANK | POSITION | SIGNATURE | DATE (YYYYMMDD)

SENIOR RATER'S ORGANIZATION | BRANCH | SENIOR RATER TELEPHONE NUMBER | E-MAIL ADDRESS (.gov or .mil)

d. This is a referred report, do you wish to make comments? ☐ Yes, comments are attached ☐ No | e. SIGNATURE OF RATED OFFICER | DATE (YYYYMMDD)

PART III - DUTY DESCRIPTION

a. PRINCIPAL DUTY TITLE BATTERY EXECUTIVE OFFICER | b. POSITION AOC/BR

c. SIGNIFICANT DUTIES AND RESPONSIBILITIES. REFER TO PART IVa, DA FORM 67-9-1.

Executive Officer of a VULCAN/STINGER air defense battery consisting of 114 personnel, 9 Towed VULCAN systems, 20 STINGER teams, 45 associated wheeled vehicles and related support equipment with the primary mission of deploying worldwide within 18 hours to provide air defense to elements of the First Infantry Brigade, 101 Airborne Division (AASLT).

PART IV - PERFORMANCE EVALUATION - PROFESSIONALISM *(Rater)*

CHARACTER Disposition of the leader: combination of values, attributes, and skills affecting leader actions

a. ARMY VALUES *(Comments mandatory for all "NO" entries. Use PART Vb.)*

	Yes	No		Yes	No
1. HONOR: Adherence to the Army's publicly declared code of values	X		**5. RESPECT:** Promotes dignity, consideration, fairness, & EO	X	
2. INTEGRITY: Possesses high personal moral standards; honest in word and deed	X		**6. SELFLESS-SERVICE:** Places Army priorities before self	X	
3. COURAGE: Manifests physical and moral bravery	X		**7. DUTY:** Fulfills professional, legal, and moral obligations	X	
4. LOYALTY: Bears true faith and allegiance to the U.S. Constitution, the Army, the unit, and the soldier				X	

b. LEADER ATTRIBUTES / SKILLS / ACTIONS: First, mark "YES" or "NO" for each block. Second, choose a total of six that best describe the rated officer. Select one from ATTRIBUTES, two from SKILLS (Competence), and three from ACTIONS (LEADERSHIP). Place an "X" in the appropriate numbered box with optional comments in PART Vb. **Comments are mandatory in Part Vb for all "No" entries.**

b.1. *ATTRIBUTES (Select 1)* Fundamental qualities and characteristics	1. **MENTAL** [X] YES / NO — Possesses desire, will, initiative, and discipline	2. **PHYSICAL** [X] YES / NO — Maintains appropriate level of physical fitness and military bearing	3. **EMOTIONAL** [X] YES / NO — Displays self-control; calm under pressure
b.2 *SKILLS (Competence) (Select 2)* Skill development is part of self-development; prerequisite to action	1. **CONCEPTUAL** [X] YES / NO — Demonstrates sound judgment, critical/creative thinking, moral reasoning	2. **INTERPERSONAL** [X] YES / NO — Shows skill with people: coaching, teaching, counseling, motivating and empowering	3. **TECHNICAL** [X] YES / NO — Possesses the necessary expertise to accomplish all tasks and functions
	4. **TACTICAL** Demonstrates proficiency in required professional knowledge, judgment, and warfighting [X] YES / NO		

b.3. *ACTIONS (LEADERSHIP) (Select 3) Major activities leaders perform: influencing, operating, and improving*

INFLUENCING Method of reaching goals while operating / improving	1. **COMMUNICATING** [X] YES / NO — Displays good oral, written, and listening skills for individuals / groups	2. **DECISION-MAKING** [X] YES / NO — Employs sound judgment, logical reasoning and uses resources wisely	3. **MOTIVATING** [X] YES / NO — Inspires, motivates, and guides others toward mission accomplishment
OPERATING Short-term mission accomplishment	4. **PLANNING** [X] YES / NO — Develops detailed, executable plans that are feasible, acceptable, and suitable	5. **EXECUTING** [X] YES / NO — Shows tactical proficiency, meets mission standards, and takes care of people/resources	6. **ASSESSING** [X] YES / NO — Uses after-action and evaluation tools to facilitate consistent improvement
IMPROVING Long-term improvement in the Army its people and organizations	7. **DEVELOPING** [X] YES / NO — Invests adequate time and effort to develop individual subordinates as leaders	8. **BUILDING** [X] YES / NO — Spends time and resources improving teams, groups and units; fosters ethical climate	9. **LEARNING** [X] YES / NO — Seeks self-improvement and organizational growth; envisioning, adapting and leading change

c. APFT: DATE: HEIGHT: WEIGHT:

d. OFFICER DEVELOPMENT - *MANDATORY YES OR NO ENTRY FOR RATERS OF CPTs, LTs, CW2s, AND WO1s.*
WERE DEVELOPMENTAL TASKS RECORDED ON DA FORM 67-9-1a AND QUARTERLY FOLLOW-UP COUNSELINGS CONDUCTED? [X] YES / NO / NA

DA FORM 67-9, MAR 2006 PREVIOUS EDITIONS ARE OBSOLETE. Page 1 of 2 APD v3.01

NAME	SSN	PERIOD COVERED

PART V - PERFORMANCE AND POTENTIAL EVALUATION *(Rater)*

a. EVALUATE THE RATED OFFICER'S PERFORMANCE DURING THE RATING PERIOD AND HIS/HER POTENTIAL FOR PROMOTION

[X] **OUTSTANDING PERFORMANCE, MUST PROMOTE** [ ] **SATISFACTORY PERFORMANCE, PROMOTE** [ ] **UNSATISFACTORY PERFORMANCE, DO NOT PROMOTE** [ ] **OTHER** *(Explain)*

b. COMMENT ON SPECIFIC ASPECTS OF THE PERFORMANCE. REFER TO PART III, DA FORM 67-9 AND PART IVa, b, AND PART Vb, DA FORM 67-9-1.

An outstanding leader and manager, (Name) performed all of his duties as executive officer with diligence and keen attention to detail. His actions were key to this battery receiving the "Best Battery" award during each of the quarterly command inspection cycles. (Name's) awards program, information security program, and sponsorship program were rated the best in the battalion. He could always be counted on to ensure all administrative requirements of the battery were completed timely and accurately. On several occasions, he assumed the duty as acting commander and performed outstandingly. (Name) is exceptionally physically fit as can be attested by the results he achieved at the Jungle Operations Training Center in Panama. He welcomes challenge and aggressively pursues both new objectives and better ways of accomplishing routine tasks. An outstanding, well-rounded officer.

c. COMMENT ON POTENTIAL FOR PROMOTION.

Ready to command a battery today—give him a tough one, he'll make it outstanding. Always promote below the zone and school ahead of competition.

d. IDENTIFY ANY UNIQUE PROFESSIONAL SKILLS OR AREAS OF EXPERTISE OF VALUE TO THE ARMY THAT THIS OFFICER POSSESSES. FOR ARMY COMPETITIVE CATEGORY CPT ALSO INDICATE A POTENTIAL CAREER FIELD FOR FUTURE SERVICE.

(Name) possesses an outstanding technical background that would support assignments in the US Army acquisition community.

PART VI - INTERMEDIATE RATER

PART VII -SENIOR RATER

a. EVALUATE THE RATED OFFICER'S PROMOTION POTENTIAL TO THE NEXT HIGHER GRADE

I currently senior rate ______________ officer(s) in this grade

A completed DA Form 67-9-1 was received with this report and considered in my evaluation and review [ ] YES [ ] NO *(Explain in c)*

[X] **BEST QUALIFIED** [ ] **FULLY QUALIFIED** [ ] **DO NOT PROMOTE** [ ] **OTHER** *(Explain below)*

b. POTENTIAL COMPARED WITH OFFICERS SENIOR RATED IN SAME GRADE (OVERPRINTED BY DA)

[X] ABOVE CENTER OF MASS (Less than 50% in top box; Center of Mass if 50% or more in top box)

[ ] CENTER OF MASS

[ ] BELOW CENTER OF MASS RETAIN

[ ] BELOW CENTER OF MASS DO NOT RETAIN

c. COMMENT ON PERFORMANCE/POTENTIAL

Outstanding officer in all aspects. The best executive officer I have ever seen. Leads by selfless example which generates undivided loyalty from all. His unit has the highest administrative and logistics readiness standards in the battalion. The unit's maintenance program is the model for others to emulate. Promote ahead of peers, send to advanced schooling early, and then place him in command.

d. LIST THREE FUTURE ASSIGNMENTS FOR WHICH THIS OFFICER IS BEST SUITED.
FOR ARMY COMPETITIVE CATEGORY CPT, ALSO INDICATE A POTENTIAL CAREER FIELD FOR FUTURE SERVICE.

Company Command, Battalion and Brigade Staff

DA FORM 67-9, MAR 2006 Page 2 of 2
APD v3.01

In Part IIc of the OER you fill in the rank and position of the senior rater. A simple rule is that higher rank generally means greater creditability. So, if possible, rather than senior rate a particularly outstanding officer under your command, ask your rater to senior rate the individual. Explain to him your reasons. Most senior raters have no objection to accelerating a young superstar. Before asking your senior rater to rate this individual, be prepared to provide proposed senior rater comments.

Keep it simple when you fill in the individual's duty title (Part IIIa). Use recognizable terms such as S4 or division plans officer, and avoid vague terms like coordinator and developer. If necessary, add extra information to the duty title line (as space permits) to further clarify a duty position. For example, assistant S1 could become Assistant S1, Divisional Fire Support Battalion.

Use Part IIIc for the individual's duty description. "The first sentence," report most board members, "is what I read." Board members read the remaining sentences if time permits, but these sentences don't have the impact of the first sentence. Mark Twain said, "The importance of using the right word is like the difference between the words lightning and lightning bug." So take the time to use the correct descriptive words that include an action verb such as lead, coordinate, or distribute, etc. The point being is that you want the prospective board member to develop a clear image of what your rated officer actually does so there is a personal connection with your rated officer.

Part IV provides you an opportunity to rate the individual's professionalism. Mark sections IVa and IVb all yes unless you have a subordinate with a problem that you must report. For example, there are officers who lie, cheat and steal. I once had a young lieutenant in my first command that had a serious drug and alcohol problem. This problem caused him to connive with a supply clerk to sell equipment on the black market and use the money to buy drugs. This case is an extreme example, but I've even seen company grade officers try to forge changes on their OER's. Yes, I am talking about using correction fluid to improve their ratings. Bottom line is that if you have someone under your command whose character is in question, rate him as such. Don't hide character flaws.

Not all commissioned officers have the necessary attributes to lead others. In my commissioning class, we had an individual who was an absolute brilliant physicist. Truly one of the most intellectually capable individuals I've ever met. However, due to a sheltered upbringing, his interpersonal skills were awful. As such, he was unable to successfully function as a leader of Soldiers. For the benefit of both the Army and the individual, it was best this person find another career that would leverage his brilliance.

Height and weight, as well as an Army Physical Fitness Test pass, are important. Why is this so important? Well, it has been proven throughout the millennia that war is an endeavor for both young and fit men. Men in poor physical condition cannot endure the mental and physical stresses of the profession. More importantly, men in leadership positions in poor physical conditions can and will cause unnecessary casualties under their command. The US Army needs not only men of character, but they need men of character who can execute operations under the most stressing of environments.

In less than a minute the prospective board member finishes reading the first page, he has sketched a mental image of the rated officer. He has determined whether or not the rated officer is a leader type. Is he fit? Can he communicate? This is the first impression. It's important that you read your draft OERs with this in mind. Critique yourself. Have you accurately portrayed the image of this officer?

Examine the sample OER. What is your image of this officer? Would a prospective board member put him on the promote list at this point? If so, where on his merit list? Upper third, middle third, or lower third?

The back page of the OER adds color and clarity to the sketch formed from the information on the front page. The critical back page determines the officer's final evaluation. Starting with Part Va, what do the blocks really mean? You might logically interpret the far left block (Outstanding Performance, Must Promote) as an above average officer, the next block (Satisfactory Performance, Promote) and an average officer and the far right blocks as different degrees of below average. Do not check any of the blocks to the right unless you intend to discredit the rated officer. Showing improvement is not a valid notion on an OER board. Members see this as a less than satisfactory performance. The Other block only applies under special circumstances, such as retirement. See appropriate regulations before checking this block.

Take care—your good intentions may easily hurt an officer.

Board members do not normally read the rater's narrative (Part Vb) in its entirety, so first and last sentences are the most important. Use the first sentence to make a broad statement of the officer's abilities and accomplishments. My adjectives, in descending order of competency, are perfect, outstanding, superb, exemplary, excellent, good, satisfactory, fair, and failed. Your actual interpretations and use of these adjectives may vary, but generally follow the above pattern.

The last sentence or two should sum up the officer's overall performance and capabilities. I've given two examples on the next page of how to emphasize the first and last sentences of the rater's narrative. The potential blocks (Part Vc & Vd) carry the rater's greatest impact on the rated officer. Like the performance blocks, the board members' interpretation of the potential block varies, but I'll describe the some accepted norms:

You can choose to say promote ahead of contemporaries. As such a board member could interpret this comment to vary the rating of the officer from a perfect to an excellent officer depending on the potential comments you supply. You must substantiate this recommendation with something the board member can relate to or he will consider it an inflationary OER that should be moved down in the merit list. For example, show an example of the rated officer success in an operation or exercise that clearly involved responsibilities far beyond his position.

To say promote with contemporaries implies "promote only if the numbers allow it; screen the officer's entire record carefully." These officers are clearly the middle of the pack or lower

RATER'S NARRATIVE EMPHASIS

EXAMPLE 1

First sentence: (Name) is the most outstanding officer I have ever witnessed in my 18 years of commissioned service. (Name) excels in all professional attributes. He combines flawless integrity, strong character, physical and mental toughness, superb perception, a balanced approach, profound sense of duty, abundant loyalty and sound judgement to accomplish each and every task in an outstanding manner.

Last Sentence: (Name) combines the drive, discipline and intellectual powers of a born commander.

EXAMPLE 2

First sentence: (Name) is the most outstanding officer I have ever known.

Last Sentence: He is a complete professional who consistently sets the example and is admire by his superiors, peers and subordinates. (Name) is a natural leader and a very bright officer who accomplishes everything outstandingly.

Do not promote means "show cause why this officer should remain in the service."

Only by writing "promote ahead of contemporaries" will you ensure the rated officer's image isn't damaged.

Previous board members that I've interviewed tell me that they only read intermediate ratings (Part VI) because of their rarity. When an intermediate rating pops up on the screen, board members are naturally curious. As a rule, however, intermediate raters do not carry much weight in the evaluation process.

The senior rater is the true heavyweight in the OER evaluation. One axiom, credited to a former board member, states, "A rated officer cannot receive a max OER without a senior rater." The heavy discriminators in the OER are in the two relatively small blocks in the senior rater portion (VIIa and VIIb). The senior rater profile and the senior rater narrative can clarify or skew the OER picture. The conscientious senior rater understands the importance and responsibility of his position. After several decades of use, I believe a few senior rater norms have developed. The most important of these is that senior raters have decided to use either above center of mass and center of mass distribution.

The essential element for any senior rater in selecting a distribution style and block is consistency. Once you've established a rating philosophy, stay the course. Over time, however, circumstances may arise that inflate your profile. In this case, it is better to restart your profile than to unnecessarily hurt a rated officer.

Effective senior rater narratives (VIIc) contain comments about the rated officer's outstanding duty performance. A qualifier such as *best* or *first* will differentiate the water walker from the above average performer. Comments about the officer's character can weigh heavily in his favor if he is equal to his peers in all other areas. As a matter of course, include the following items in a good rating: promote immediately, send to advanced schooling now, place in the next level of command now, (name) is a candidate to work at the highest echelons of the Army.

The above average senior rater criteria are the different colors of paint you need to complete the OER masterpiece. Now sit back and view your latest subordinate OER to determine if you are sending all the correct messages to the prospective board members. The last thing a rater wishes is to unintentionally hurt an outstanding young subordinate.

SENIOR RATER PROFILE

Four-Block Spread

Top block: Walks on water; one or two out of a hundred. Promote below the zone, send immediately to the next higher school, entrust with the toughest and choicest assignment.

Second block: Top officer, better than average, promote, consider below the zone, send to higher schools.

Third block: Average officer, promote with peers, consider for advanced schooling.

Fourth block: Below average, do not promote.

TYPICAL RATING SCHEME

Rank	Officer	Duty Position	Rater	Inter Rater	Sr Rater	Next OER
LTC	FLAG	BN CDR	COL STEEL	BG HAMMER	MG TOUGH	120110
MAJ	BUZZ	BN XO	LTC FLAG		COL STEEL	120110
MAJ	STATIC	BN S3	LTC FLAG		COL STEEL	110723
CPT	BAND	XCO CDR	LTC FLAG		COL STEEL	120312
CPT	WAVE	ZCO, CDR	LTC FLAG		COL STEEL	121215
CPT	SWITCH	HQ CO, CDR	LTC FLAG		COL STEEL	121214
CPT	PAPER	BN S1	MAJ BUZZ		LTC FLAG	120219
CPT	JUNK	BN S4	MAJ BUZZ		LTC FLAG	110316
CPT	SLACK	ASST S3	MAJ STATIC		LTC FLAG	120521
1LT	SMARTY	BN S2	MAJ BUZZ		LTC FLAG	110331
1LT	BRIGHT	XCO,XO	CPT BAND		LTC FLAG	121022
1LT	SHARP	ZCO,XO	CPT WAVE		LTC FLAG	120301
2LT	NET	1/X CO, PL	CPT BAND		LTC FLAG	110228
2LT	LOST	2/X CO, PL	CPT BAND		LTC FLAG	110513
2LT	HERO	1/Z CO, PL	CPT WAVE		LTC FLAG	120201
2LT	ZERO	2/Z CO, PL	CPT WAVE		LTC FLAG	120302

CHAPTER FOUR

Command and Leadership Resources

As the advice and stories outlined in Chapter One and Two indicate, leadership development is a journey. A journey each one of you young officers need to take whether you decide to make the military a career or not. I assure you that you *will* use those fundamental leadership skills developed and matured during your time in the military on a daily basis in whatever career you might choose after the military.

One of the key and important resources during your military career is your contemporaries. Yes, your contemporaries. I know what you're thinking. *"How can I learn from my fellow officers? I'm competing with them for a discriminating OER. They won't help me and I certainly don't feel comfortable helping them."*

Help them you must. You are in the profession of arms. The lives of your Soldiers, your contemporaries, and their Soldiers depend on competent, informed, and focused leadership. This brotherhood and the safety of your Soldiers are supremely more important than any OER.

I know in the last chapter I discussed the importance of writing a proper OER and the effect of your command OERs on your career. Let me give you the same advice I've given every Lieutenant or Captain who has ever worked for me. That is "Just do the best of your ability in everything you do." I have found that when a young officer does the best of his/her ability, he will succeed more times than he will fail. Yes, you will fail. That isn't what is important. What is important is what you do *after* you fail. Remember from Chapter One, will is more important than talent. Your must learn from that failure and make it right. You make it right by constantly improving your skills and leadership abilities. At rating time, no matter what happens, you can feel comfortable that you gave it your best. You will have nothing to be ashamed of. Just as important, you've helped your contemporaries to be their best for the same reasons.

MILSPACE

The first source I want to mention to help you young platoon leaders and company commanders interact and develop is a website entitled MILSPACE. This website offers a number of different ways to access and exchange experiences with your fellow officers. Two important components I would like to introduce are the Company Command and Platoon Leader forums. The URLs are listed below:

http://PL.army.mil

http://CC.army.mil

In these forums platoon leaders and company grade officers interact on any and all subjects related to their duties. The Company Command forum is also published as a regular column in ARMY Magazine. The following pages contain an such an article, each section written by one of your contemporaries. These testimonies demonstrate that there are many leadership styles that promote success in the US Army. However, you will also be able to discern common leader characteristics, values and maybe techniques that work. Take good ideas from your contemporaries and use what fits your leadership style and comfort level. Whatever you adopt from another, make it yours and make it authentic.

Christopher Collins

B/309th

The three biggest influences on my becoming a good commander were role modeling, developmental experiences and professional reading. When I was enlisted, my first commander made it a priority to come in on the weekend and sign my emergency leave form. I've never forgotten what that meant to me, and I draw on that experience whenever I'm dealing with Soldiers who are in critical or emergency situations. When I was a lieutenant, I worked for three company commanders who were professionals and who assisted in my development for company command. One commander displayed trust in my abilities and recommended me for challenging positions in the company and a later job in HHC (Headquarters and Headquarters Company). The second commander allowed me, as a platoon leader, to develop and implement plans/ He used "outside the box" techniques and was a lead-by-example officer. The third commander required me to develop platoon training schedules, which at the time was painful but later helped me develop training schedules as a company commander. Professional reading has also been instrumental to my development. Before I took command, a friend and mentor recommended I read *Taking the Guidon*. I applied certain techniques emphasized in it while in command. It's a model for conducting training meetings was especially valuable to my unit's effectiveness.

Richard Moyers

C/2-35 IN & HHC/2-35 IN

Becoming a good commander is the result of forging process, if you will.

First, the raw materials are the talents that we bring to the table. Our personal attributes such as courage, candor, intuition, likelihood to research, and personal skills bring us to and through pre-commissioning and commissioning. Then our raw materials are beaten, heated, cooled, and shaped my master crafters and influencers. Previous commanders beat on us to become better during our lieutenant days ; peers heat and cool us during the days and nights from pre-commissioning through staff; the shaping is done by trusted mentors, loved ones/family members, and the backbone of our Army—NCOs. What emerges is the sword of our command. I had a great first platoon sergeant (PSG) when I was a platoon leader. He was the proverbial old, salty PSG. Near retirement, he seemed larger than life, but he knew and accepted his responsibility to keep me humble yet empower me to make decisions. As the twig is bent, so grows the tree. As an executive officer (XO), I struggled and was put under constant "flame" by my commander. He was immensely demanding, tireless in pushing me toward perfection and dedicated to ensuring that I could carry on in case he couldn't. Though this was a painful process, it was ultimately required.

The Captains Career Course was a cooling period. After three years of beating and heat, being allowed to cool while exchanging peer experiences, learning new doctrinal tools, and preparing for staff was incredibly valuable. It was also a great time to reflect upon those things I'd experience as a lieutenant.

Then came the crucible of staff. Staff time was important because it is when I learned about the forest, not just the trees.

Once in command, my learning didn't stop. During my first command, my three greatest influences were my wife (then-girlfriend), my 1SG (who had been one of my Ranger instructors when I was a young 2LT) and my S-3. Sounding boards, each of them helped me to see things like family issues, single-Soldier issues, and how our company affected those to the left and right of us.

Patrick McCarthy

A/9th PSYOP BN (ABN)

I try never to think that I am "good". Instead, I like to think that I am getting better each day at what I do. Way back, "in the day," I was introduced to the Principles of Leadership, and the first bullet point, "know yourself and seek self-improvement" resonated with me. Inspired by that principle, I adopted a "lifelong learning approach" that has served me well. I have strived to be a well-informed, positive leader who continues to learn, keeps faith with my Soldiers, tolerates well-intentioned mistakes and is honest.

I've always tried to be a well-informed officer—abreast if developing news situations, well-read in doctrine and a conversationalist with like-minded contemporaries. I found that by surrounding myself with professionals, I was more likely to become a well rounded leader with a kit bag full of trusted experience. I also had a sounding board for ideas and concepts. Positive attitude: I adopted a glass-half-full perspective, choosing to be an optimist and to maintain a can-do attitude. I believe that people adopt the personality of their leader and that a positive leader creates a positive, more effective unit. Continuous learning: I record everything that works well and that does not work well. This system has proved invaluable to me, from my days as a fire-team leader to now as a company commander. Unfortunately for my wife, I have volumes of green memorandum books marked "Leadership Lessons and Observations" that make no sense to anyone but myself. I read a lot and try to apply what has been written to my current challenges. Faith: I put my faith, trust and confidence in my subordinates. I empowered NCOs to conduct day-to-day business, and I beat into my lieutenants' heads to think and plan. I cultivated relationships with my first sergeants. I always kept my ears open and was willing to adopt subordinates' recommendations.

Tolerance: I would not be effective as a leader, let alone a company commander, had my previous leaders not underwritten my mistakes as learning experiences. I have carried that philosophy with me and continue to pay it forward. I do have some "big rocks" that I won't compromise on, but on almost everything else, I can work with and continue to shape, mold, and develop those who are worth investment. Honestly, I like to think I am honest with myself, my peers and those I lead. I encourage candid comments and don't take them personally in front of Soldiers. I do want their feedback, and I want to improve every day. I like to think that as long as I keep doing these things, perhaps one day I will be "good" and continue to have an impact on the great profession we are serving.

Jeff O'Dell

F/2-10 AV (Pathfinder)

I was raised on a farm. Working on a farm, you learn that things sometimes go wrong and that whining about a problem doesn't solve it, so you might as well work to find a practical solution and keep moving forward. I remember once, when I was a 14 year-old, the manure spreader that I was operating jammed up. I went and told my grandfather. He turned to me and replied in a matter-of-factly, "Well, scrape off the manure, see what's wrong and get it working again." Just like that. So I went out and did what needed to be done. Time and again in my career, I've faced situations that just stunk (though not so literally), whether it was an unexpected boulder on our helicopter landing zone or the sudden loss of a key leader. Understanding that dwelling on misfortune doesn't solve the problem, I knew that it was my job as a leader to focus my Soldiers on what needed to be done, not on what had happened. I think that this practical, solutions-focused approach helped my unit overcome some very difficult situations.

Another important experience for me was Ranger School. Yes, I learned some important tactical skills—how to set in an ambush, troop-learning procedures, etc. But the most important skills I developed there were intangible, interpersonal ones. I learned how to influence exhausted, hungry Soldiers to continue marching mile after mile, to stay awake on an ambush line, to do all things required to accomplish the mission and to take pride in themselves. In short, I learned that leadership in difficult situations is all about relating to people effectively.

When I was appointed my battalion's scout platoon leader in Iraq, the commander gave me the mission to take down the enemy's IED (improvised explosive device) cells operating in our area of operations (AO). My battalion was "eating" an IED a day, and lot of guys were earning Purple Hearts. I did what I knew how to do. I laid out the problem, made some assumptions, and began collecting data on where and when the IEDs were detonating. Within a few weeks, I had enough data to identify patterns and to create a template for the time and location of a likely IED emplacement. We set in a sniper kill team, and sure enough, the bad guys showed up. A sniper rifle and a SAW (squad automatic weapon) put an end to four of them that night.

Immediately, the rate of IEDs in our AO decreased from one a day to one a week. Soon, we successfully targeted another location and took out another IED team, and our IED problem was solved. A few years later, when I was a commander, I noticed that the lieutenants who were the best problem solvers were folks who had majored in engineering in college. This helped me realize that my own degree in Aeronautical Engineering was serving me well. Engineering is all about problem solving; so is leadership.

Darrell Fawley

C/1-23 IN

I don't know that there is a clear answer to the question of when I became a good platoon leader. Even as a current company commander, I am still learning about how to lead a platoon. It's a continuous journey.

I graduated Ranger School and thought, "I'm really good at OPORDs (operations orders) and tactics. I'm going to be a great PL!" Then I arrived at my first unit and got hit with a whole bunch of discipline issues. We fixed them, and I started noticing myself making decisions and I thought, "Wow, I'm making decision without over-thinking. I'm doing pretty well." Then we started going to the range, and I realized I still had much to learn.

Later on, we started doing good PT (physical training), and Soldiers were motivated. The commander and I were in sync, and everything was pointing to us being the company's best platoon. I thought, "We're the best, and that means I'm the best." Then we deployed and came across a lot of unexpected terrain and a tough enemy situation, and I realized I was still immature and learning. The platoon started getting better on the ground through experience, and we refined our systems. We got to a point where we could execute any mission without too much hassle. We had systems in place that were airtight, and everyone in the platoon brought ideas on how to conduct our outpost defense better, patrol better, train better, etc. I thought, "This is it. We've arrived, and I really know what I'm doing."

About that time, I took over an antiarmor platoon and realized that I knew very little about its tactics or equipment. But, I thought, "I'm a great platoon leader and can whip this platoon in shape." Over the next 10 months, I did more learning than teaching and saw tactics and techniques that we hadn't used in my rifle platoon. However, after a while the platoon could search a house in the middle of the night without waking up the inhabitants and set up on a rooftop to conduct an

OP (observation post), or navigate through the farm fields and set up an ambush with ease. I believed we were the company's best platoon, and I thought that I was finally where I needed to be as a lieutenant. At the end of the deployment, I thought I had learned all I need to learn about being a PL, so I went to MCCC (Maneuver Captains Career Course) as a 1LT and then was assigned to be an IBOLC (Infantry Basic Officer Leadership Course) platoon trainer. Every cycle I went through, I learned as I taught. At the end of every class, I'd think, "I would be the best platoon leader in the battalion now." I left IBOLC thinking there was no more to learn about being a PL. Then I worked in the brigade S-3 shop for 6 weeks and talked with other former rifle platoon leaders, and they taught me so much more. Now I'm in command, and I am still learning about being a good PL.

For me, mentorship, training and reading all the set the base, but "becoming good" is a continued learning process that will never be over. There is always more to learn about orders, weapons employment, training, fitness and a multitude of other things.

Frank Slavin III

HHT/4-9 CAV

As cringe worthy as it sounds, before taking command I spent a lot of time on staff. I eventually took command while in combat. Luckily, I had had five months as the squadron's battle captain to observe and understand the squadron's battlespace in Baghdad. Once I had the guidon in hand, and for the next three years over two commands, I relied on my 1SGs, PSGs and other subordinates to make our troop function well. My 1SGs and I talked daily—almost all day, sometimes—about what was going on in the troop, what things we/I could do better, what was on the right track and how we should capture it for later use. Three of my 1SGs and I had an awesome battle-buddy command relationship, which proved to be invaluable when things hit the fan. I mentored my XOs to do my job. In fact, my last XO was so squared away with the daily business of the troop that I probably could have commanded from my living room during the final four months I was in command.

I was also blessed to have some of the best S-3s, XOs, operations SGMs and commanders to look up to. Every one of these men would take time to talk me through what they saw as success at the troop level, both before and after I took command. Without some outstanding mentors taking an active role in teaching me, I think I would have had a much harder time.

I never considered myself to be so good that I could kick back and relax; I looked forward to each day as a new learning experience. There was always a situation when talking with peers, subordinates or superiors when the light bulb would come on and I would have that "ah-ha" moment, thus increasing my already bursting kit bag.

Steven Delvaux

A/2-187 IN

We're all products of our experiences, and everything factors into making us who we are and helping us become more effective as leaders and commanders.

I had a loving and supportive wife and family. I had a great relationship with God and that imbued me with love, patience, humility, wisdom and understanding for my Soldiers. I had great friends and fellow commanders whom I could vet with. I had a great battalion commander who taught me. I learned a ton of lessons while I was a platoon leader and XO, and I kept my eyes and ears open. I had an awesome company commander when I was a PL who taught me by personal example. I carpooled and had lunch with Tony Burgess every day at the Captains Career Course, and we shared our experiences and talked a lot about the great (and not so great) company commanders we had as PLs. I was open to accepting that my way wasn't the only way, nor was it always the best way. I had absolutely superior PLs who did the lion's share of the lifting on all the heavy work. I listened. I cared. I always gave 100 percent. I tried always to lead from the front and share all my Soldier's privations, I had great 1SGs, great NCOs and great Soldiers. I was willing to sacrifice. I tried always to be selfless. I loved the unit and my Soldiers, and I really, really, really believed in our mission. I stressed the importance of teamwork. I paid attention to the little stuff—maintenance, supply, etc.—the devil is always in the details. I owned it—took responsibility for everything my unit failed to do and always tried to defer the praise to my Soldiers when I got credit for something good. You know, it all just kind of came together.

Everything that we do counts. No man can survive in a vacuum, and no man is an island. We're all products of our experiences, and if we're paying attention, holing ourselves accountable, working as a team, emulating the Warrior Ethos and Army Values, leading in accordance with the Leadership Dimensions as outlined in FM- 6-22 (*Army Leadership*), and trying to get better every day, then we will survive and be effective company commanders. I firmly believe it.

It seems pretty clear that we take responsibility for our own learning while recognizing that much of that learning occurs through interactions with our fellow professionals—mentors, peers, subordinates—in both formal and informal settings.

The Army can live on short rations, it can be insufficiently clothed and housed, it can even be poorly armed and equipped, but it is doomed to destruction without the trained and adequate leadership if its officers. An efficient and sufficient corps of officers means the difference between victory and defeat.

—*Gen. Douglas MacArthur*

Read2Lead

Another MILSPACE study resource that is available to young officers is a program called Read2Lead. Read2Lead is a list of books that have made a difference to those platoon leaders and/or company commanders serving today. Recommend you participate at the following URL.

http://read2lead.army.mil

As part of the Read2Lead program you do the following:

1. **VOTE** on the books that have actually made a difference for you personally (books move up a notch in the list when you vote).
2. **COMMENT** and share a couple sentences specifically about how the book made a difference for you.
3. **RECOMMEND** a book (if not yet on the list) that made a difference for you as a PLT LDR or CO CDR. Keep it short (3-5 sentences) and in the first person. Talk about how it made a practical impact for you, not why others should read it.

Your vote will generate a new interactive reading recommendation list that becomes *the* profession's reading list for company-level leaders.

My personal reading list favorites are:

The Art of War, Sun Tzu

Alexander the Great, Robin Lane Fox

Napoleon, Felix Markham

The Autobiography of Ulysses S Grant, Ulysses S Grant

Killer Angels, Michael Shaara

There are many excellent books that deserve mention. However, my focus has mainly been on reading biographies and autobiographies of the great leaders.

Leader Cast

The last resource from MILSPACE I wish to mention is
Leader Cast: Think "YouTube" inside MilSpace.
There are over 800 video clips of leaders sharing their experience. Using key words, you can find a pertinent video with one click.

CHAPTER FIVE

Contributing to the Institution of the United States Army

Of all the institutions in the United States of America, the United States Army is one of the most respected. It is respected because it has been able to consistently maintain a high standard of moral values and operations success. The US Army has also been able to successfully integrate people from all walks of life for the last two centuries into the fiercest fighting force in the world. The "institution" of the US Army is one of the most valuable in this country. It consistently produces leaders of character at all ranks and ages that eventually leave the Army to use their talents in other professions of service for our country and communities. It is important that current and former Soldiers work together to improve and protect the institution of the US Army. The Association of the United States Army (AUSA) is an organization that enables current and former Soldiers to work together for the long term greater good of the US Army. Specifically, since 1950 AUSA has worked to support all aspects of national security while advancing the interests of America's Army and the men and women who serve. AUSA is a private, non-profit educational organization that supports America's Army - Active, National Guard, Reserve, Civilians, Retirees, Government Civilians, Wounded Warriors, Veterans, and family members.

AUSA has 125 chapters located worldwide. Made up entirely of volunteers, they provide recreational and educational opportunities to Soldiers and their families. Most importantly, they support our deployed Soldiers and families left behind. AUSA and its' chapters have contributed over $2,000,000 to awards, scholarships, and support of Soldier and family programs.

Grassroots support for America's Army can only come when people know and understand the value of the Army to the nation. AUSA accomplishes this through its various chapters, the Institute for Land Warfare, Industry Affairs meeting and events, and its Government Affairs office. As an Army professional, you need to keep current on issues that affect you in the work place. AUSA offers educational material and events designed specifically to educate you about these issues.

I believe in this organization and serve on the Board of Directors for my local chapter. I don't recommend active duty Soldiers serve as a Chapter Officer due to the significant volunteer time involved, however, young officers can volunteer and assist on specific events in your military community.

AUSA is open to all Army ranks and all components—including Active, National Guard, Army Reserve—Government civilians, retirees, Wounded Warriors, Veterans, concerned citizens and family members.

REFERENCES

AR 11-33 .... ARMY LESSONS LEARNED PROGRAM (ALLP)

AR 15-6........................ PROCEDURES FOR INVESTIGATING OFFICERS AND BOARDS OF

AR 15-185 .... ARMY BOARD FOR CORRECTION OF MILITARY RECORDS

AR 25-50 .... PREPARING AND MANAGING CORRESPONDENCE

PAM 25-40.................. ARMY PUBLISHING: ACTION OFFICERS GUIDE

AR 27-10 .... MILITARY JUSTICE

AR 37-104-4 .... MILITARY PAY AND ALLOWANCES POLICY

AR 135-155 .... PROMOTION OF COMMISSIONED OFFICERS AND WARRANT OFFICERS OTHER THAN GENERAL OFFICERS

AR 135-175 .... SEPARATION OF OFFICERS

AR 135-178 .... ENLISTED ADMINISTRATIVE SEPARATIONS

AR 135-205 .... ENLISTED PERSONNEL MANAGEMENT

AR 190-9 .... ABSENTEE DESERTER APPREHENSION PROGRAM AND SURRENDER OF MILITARY PERSONNEL TO CIVILIAN LAW ENFORCEMENT AGENCIES

AR 190-16 .... PHYSICAL SECURITY

AR 220-45 .... DUTY ROSTERS

AR 350-1 .... ARMY TRAINING AND LEADER DEVELOPMENT

AR 381-12 .... SUBVERSION AND ESPIONAGE DIRECTED AGAINST THE U.S. ARMY (SAEDA)

AR 385-10 .... THE ARMY SAFETY PROGRAM

AR 385-63 .... RANGE SAFETY

PAM 385-1.................. SMALL UNIT SAFETY OFFICER/NCO GUIDE

PAM 385-10 .... ARMY SAFETY PROGRAM

PAM 385-40 .... ARMY ACCIDENT INVESTIGATIONS AND REPORTING

PAM 385-63 .... RANGE SAFETY

AR 600-8-2 .... SUSPENSION OF FAVORABLE PERSONNEL ACTIONS (FLAGS)

AR 600-8-4 .... LINE OF DUTY POLICY, PROCEDURES, AND INVESTIGATIONS

AR 600-8-6 .... PERSONNEL ACCOUNTING AND STRENGTH REPORTING

AR 600-8-10 .... LEAVES AND PASSES

AR 600-8-11 .... REASSIGNMENT

AR 600-8-19 .... ENLISTED PROMOTIONS AND REDUCTIONS

AR 600-8-22 .... MILITARY AWARDS

AR 600-8-24 .... OFFICER TRANSFER AND DISCHARGES

AR 600-8-29 .... OFFICER PROMOTIONS

AR 600-9 .... THE ARMY WEIGHT CONTROL PROGRAM

AR 600-15 .... INDEBTEDNESS OF MILITARY PERSONNEL

AR 600-20 .... ARMY COMMAND POLICY

AR 600-25 .... SALUTES, HONORS, AND VISITS OF COURTESY

AR 600-37 .... UNFAVORABLE INFORMATION

AR 600-43 .... CONSCIENTIOUS OBJECTION

AR 600-100 .... ARMY LEADERSHIP

PAM 600-15 .... EXTREMIST ACTIVITIES

PAM 600-25 .... U.S. ARMY NONCOMMISSIONED OFFICER PROFESSIONAL DEVELOPMENT GUIDE

PAM 600-35 .... RELATIONSHIPS BETWEEN SOLDIERS OF DIFFERENT RANKS

PAM 600-60 .... A GUIDE TO PROTOCOL AND ETIQUETTE FOR OFFICIAL ENTERTAINMENT

PAM 600-65 .... LEADERSHIP - STATEMENTS AND QUOTES

PAM 600-85 .... ARMY SUBSTANCE ABUSE PROGRAM CIVILIAN SERVICES

AR 601-280 .... ARMY RETENTION PROGRAM

AR 608-1 .... ARMY COMMUNITY SERVICE CENTER

AR 608-18 .... THE ARMY FAMILY ADVOCACY PROGRAM

AR 608-20 .... ARMY VOTING ASSISTANCE PROGRAM

AR 608-47 .... ARMY FAMILY ACTION PLAN (ACAP) PROGRAM

AR 608-48 .... ARMY FAMILY TEAM BUILDING (AFTB) PROGRAM

AR 608-75 .... EXCEPTIONAL FAMILY MEMBER PROGRAM

AR 608-99 .... FAMILY SUPPORT, CHILD CUSTODY, AND PATERNITY

AR 614-11 .... TEMPORARY DUTY (TDY)

AR 623-3 .... EVALUATION REPORTING SYSTEM

PAM 623-3.................. EVALUATION REPORTING SYSTEM

AR 630-10 .... ABSENCE WITHOUT LEAVE, DESERTION, AND ADMINISTRATION OF PERSONNEL INVOLVED IN CIVILIAN COURT PROCEEDINGS

AR 635-5 .... SEPARATION DOCUMENTS

AR 635-200 .... ACTIVE DUTY ENLISTED ADMINISTRATIVE SEPARATIONS

PAM 640-1.................. OFFICERS' GUIDE TO THE OFFICER RECORD BRIEF

AR 670-1 .... WEAR AND APPEARANCE OF ARMY UNIFORMS AND INSIGNIA

AR 700-132 .... JOINT OIL ANALYSIS PROGRAM

PAM 735-5.................. FINANCIAL LIABILITY OFFICER'S GUIDE

AR 840-10 .... FLAGS, GUIDONS, STREAMERS, TABARDS, AND AUTOMOBILE AND AIRCRAFT PLATES

AR 870-5 .... MILITARY HISTORY: RESPONSIBILITIES, POLICIES AND PROCEDURES

AR 930-4 .... ARMY EMERGENCY RELIEF

AR 930-5 .... AMERICAN NATIONAL RED CROSS SERVICE PROGRAM AND ARMY UTILIZATION

FM 1-05...................... RELIGIOUS SUPPORT SS FM 16-1 18-Apr-03

FM 1-20...................... MILITARY HISTORY OPERATIONS 3-Feb-03

FM 3-0........................ OPERATIONS 27-Feb-08

FM 3-05.70................. SURVIVAL SS FM 21-76 17-May-02

FM 3-06...................... URBAN OPERATIONS 26-Oct-06

FM 3-06.20................. CORDON AND SEARCH MULTI-SERVICE TACTICS, TECHNIQUES, AND PROCEDURES FOR CORDON AND SEARCH OPERATIONS 25-Apr-06

FM 3-07...................... STABILITY OPERATIONS 6-Oct-08

FM 3-19.30................. PHYSICAL SECURITY SS FM 19-30 8-Jan-01

FM 3-21.5................... DRILL AND CEREMONIES CHANGE 1, 12 APRIL 2006 7-Jul-03

FM 3-22.9................... RIFLE MARKSMANSHIP M16-/M4-SERIES WEAPONS 12-Aug-08

FM 3-22.27................. MK 19, 40-MM GRENADE MACHINE GUN, MOD 3 CHANGE 1, 14 SEP 2006 28-Nov-03

FM 3-22.31................. 40-MM GRENADE LAUNCHER, M203 CHANGE 1, 19 MARCH 2007 13-Feb-03

FM 3-22.65................. BROWNING MACHINE GUN CALIBER .50 HB, M2 CHANGE 1, 11 APRIL 2007 3-Mar-05

FM 3-22.68................. CREW-SERVED MACHINE GUNS 5.56-MM AND 7.62-MM 21-Jul-06

FM 3-23.30................. GRENADES AND PYROTECHNIC SIGNALS 15-Oct-09

FM 3-24...................... COUNTERINSURGENCY 15-Dec-06

FM 3-25.26................. MAP READING AND LAND NAVIGATION CHANGE 1, 30 AUG 2006 18-Jan-05

FM 3-25.150............... COMBATIVES CONTROLLED DISTRIBUTION 1-Apr-09

FM 3-50.3................... SURVIVAL, EVASION, AND RECOVERY MULTI-SERVICE TACTICS, TECHNIQUES, AND PROCEDURES 20-Mar-07

FM 3-97.6................... MOUNTAIN OPERATIONS SS FM 90-6, 30 June 1980 28-Nov-00

FM 3-97.61................. MILITARY MOUNTAINEERING CHANGE 1, 20 FEB 2003 26-Aug-02

FM 3-100.21............... CONTRACTORS ON THE BATTLEFIELD SS FM 100-21 3-Jan-03

FM 4-0........................ SUSTAINMENT SS FM 4-0, COMBAT SERVICE SUPPORT, AUG 03 30-Apr-09

FM 4-02.51................. COMBAT AND OPERATIONAL STRESS CONTROL SS FM 8-51 6-Jul-06

FM 4-25.11................. FIRST AID CHANGE 1, 15 JULY 2004; SS FM 21-11 23-Dec-02

FM 4-25.12................. UNIT FIELD SANITATION TEAM SS FM 21-10-1, 11 October 1989 25-Jan-02

FM 4-30.3................... MAINTENANCE OPERATIONS AND PROCEDURES 28-Jul-04

FM 4-30.13................. AMMUNITION HANDBOOK: TACTICS, TECHNIQUES, AND PROCEDURES FOR MUNITIONS HANDLERS SS FM 9-13 (1986) & FM 9-38 (1993) 1-Mar-01

FM 4-30.31................. RECOVERY AND BATTLE DAMAGE ASSESSMENT AND REPAIR SS FM 9-43-2 19-Sep-06

FM 4-30.51................. UNEXPLODED ORDNANCE (UXO) PROCEDURES SS FM 21-16 13-Jul-06

FM 5-0........................ THE OPERATIONS PROCESS SS 20 JAN 05 & FMI 5-0.1

FM 5-19...................... COMPOSITE RISK MANAGEMENT SS FM 100-14 21-Aug-06

FM 5-33...................... TERRAIN ANALYSIS Ch 1, 8 Sep 92 11-Jul-90

FM 5-102.................... COUNTERMOBILITY 14-Mar-85

FM 5-103.................... SURVIVABILITY 10-Jun-85

FM 5-412.................... PROJECT MANAGEMENT 13-Jun-94

FM 7-21.13................. THE SOLDIER'S GUIDE 2-Feb-04

FM 7-22.7................... THE ARMY NONCOMMISSIONED OFFICER GUIDE SS TC 22-6 23-Dec-02

FM 20-3...................... CAMOUFLAGE, CONCEALMENT, AND DECOYS 30-Aug-99

FM 21-10.................... FIELD HYGIENE AND SANITATION 21-Jun-00

FM 21-18.................... FOOT MARCHES 1-Jun-90

FM 21-20.................... PHYSICAL FITNESS TRAINING Change 1, 1 October 1998 30-Sep-92

FM 22-6...................... GUARD DUTY Ch 1, 15 Jan 75 17-Sep-71

FM 23-23.................... ANTIPERSONNEL MINE M18A1 AND M18 (CLAYMORE) Ch 2, 30 Mar 73 6-Jan-66

FM 27-1 .... LEGAL GUIDE FOR COMMANDERS 13-Jan-92

FM 27-10 .... THE LAW OF LAND WARFARE Change 1, 15 Jul 76 18-Jul-56

FM 31-70 .... BASIC COLD WEATHER MANUAL Change 1, 17 Dec 68 12-Apr-68

FM 46-1 .... PUBLIC AFFAIRS OPERATIONS 30-May-97

GTA 01-14-001 .... BATTLE DAMAGE ASSESSMENT AND REPAIR (BDAR) SMART BOOK

GTA 05-02-013 .... HOW TO FIND YOUR WAY

GTA 05-02-034 .... AZIMUTH-BEARING/GRID-MAGNETIC CONVERSION

GTA 05-08-001 .... SURVIVABILITY POSITIONS

GTA 05-08-012 .... INDIVIDUAL SAFETY CARD

GTA 05-10-033 .... DEMOLITION CARD

GTA 07-01-036 .... DISASSEMBLY LAYOUT CHART, M9 SEMIAUTOMATIC PISTOL, 9MM

GTA 07-04-006 .... INFANTRY LEADER'S REFERENCE CARD FOR BUILDING THE COMPANY TEAM FOR DEFENSE

GTA 07-04-007 .... TRAINING MEETING

GTA 07-04-008 .... INFANTRY LEADER'S REFERENCE CARD FOR LINKUP OPERATIONS

GTA 07-06-001 .... FIGHTING POSITION CONSTRUCTION - INFANTRY LEADER'S REFERENCE CARD

GTA 07-08-003 .... PHYSICAL READINESS TRAINING QUICK REFERENCE CARD

GTA 08-11-011 .... ARTIFICIAL RESPIRATION/BASIC CARDIAC LIFE SUPPORT (CPR)

GTA 09-12-001 .... UNEXPLODED ORDNANCE (UXO) PROCEDURES

GTA 12-01-001 .... ARMY SUICIDE PREVENTION PROGRAM

GTA 21-02-008 .... THE SOLDIER'S INFORMATION GUIDE

GTA 30-02-001 .... A SOLDIER'S GUIDE TO DIRECT QUESTIONING, REPORTING AND DETAINEE OPERATIONS (ES2)

GiPubs
.COM

Recommended Reading:

THE MENTOR

Everything You Need To Know About Leadership & Counseling

For a decade, The Mentor has been considered one of the most practical and informative references available to U.S. Army Leaders. This new 10th anniversary edition has been completely renovated. The data, references, advice, and example documents that thousands have come to expect from The Mentor have all returned in force. The content, updated in accordance with current doctrine, has been reorganized for easier readability. It's new format makes it your "quick and dirty" guide for all your leadership issues.

Learn to counsel, evaluate, correct, and initiate adverse actions in a fashion that will achieve positive results. Your primary goal as a leader is to grow, shape, and mold your team to be as mission-effective as possible. Some leaders will choose to do this by brute strength or force of will. This book focuses on building a cohesive unit by following simple principles that foster good will and show your Soldiers that you care.

MOVE OUT

The Insider's Guide to Military Leaders

The Screamer. The Weasel. The Know-It-All. Do you know how to survive a work environment that is dominated by these boss archetypes? Do you know where your career is headed? Do you know how to organize yourself to meet this goal? Do you know how to recruit your colleagues to your cause and create solid allies in your workplace? Do you know how to handle "problem subordinates"? Move Out explains all this and much more. This leader handbook is the product of years of first hand experience and a keen eye for observation. This book reveals the tips, tricks, and insider knowledge that will help you unlock your true career potential in the field of military leadership. Colonel Rusin illustrates her points with numerous examples in her signature style of spot-on explanation. Move Out is a great read and an invaluable cornerstone of any military leader's library.

AUTHOR'S PARTING SHOT

I want to end this book by discussing the meaning of the word "professional." Webster's Dictionary defines it as:

- **Characterized by or conforming to the technical or ethical standards of a profession, or**
- **Following a line of conduct as though it were a profession.**

I'm sure that you've known people in your life that you would categorize as professionals who fit Webster's definition perfectly. You respect and trust them because they know their business.

I've always told the young officers who worked for me that I don't care whether they become career officers or not. I want them to give me their best and become a professional as part of their nature. A professional grows over time. A professional knows that personal experience and technical study widens his perspective providing a solid basis for actions and decisions. Wouldn't it be a compliment if people called you a professional? Personally, I can't think of a better tribute.

—FJC